More Praise for Kathy LeMay's

The *Generosity* Plan

"Kathy LeMay has helped me to determine how I am going to use my time, treasure and talent to make a difference in this world."

—JACKI ZEHNER, FORMER MANAGING PARTNER, GOLDMAN, SACHS & CO.

"Kathy grabs your attention and holds you captive throughout. . . !"

—JANICE WEISS, YWCA ANCHORAGE

"I have always believed that individual security and stability depends on all of humanity, that we are all linked. *The Generosity Plan* is a must read because it provides constructive ways we can share our time, talent, and treasure to make a positive difference in the world."

—ARUN GANDHI, PRESIDENT OF THE GANDHI WORLDWIDE EDUCATION INSTITUTE, USA, WWW.GANDHIFORCHILDREN.ORG

"[Kathy LeMay] speaks from her heart and provides clarity to the conversation around giving. . . Time spent with Kathy is an investment both in yourself and towards a better world."

—LAURA B. DAVIS, VICE PRESIDENT, JP MORGAN, THE PRIVATE BANK

". . . inspiring, authentic, and catalytic."

—NINA SIMONS, CO-EXECUTIVE DIRECTOR AND CO-PRODUCER OF BIONEERS

The
Generosity
Plan

*Sharing Your Time, Treasure, and Talent
to Shape the World*

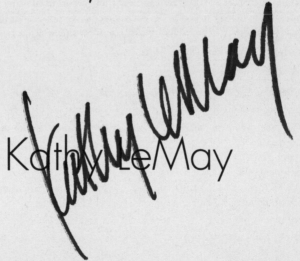

Kathy LeMay

ATRIA PAPERBACK
New York London Toronto Sydney

 BEYOND WORDS
Hillsboro, Oregon

ATRIA PAPERBACK
A Division of Simon & Schuster, Inc.
1230 Avenue of the Americas
New York, NY 10020

BEYOND WORDS
20827 N.W. Cornell Road, Suite 500
Hillsboro, Oregon 97124-9808
503-531-8700 / 503-531-8773 fax
www.beyondword.com

Managing editor: Lindsay S. Brown
Copyeditor: Ali McCart
Proofreader: Jennifer Weaver-Neist
Design: Devon Smith
Composition: William H. Brunson Typography Services

First Atria Paperback/Beyond Words trade paperback edition January 2010

ATRIA PAPERBACK and colophon are trademarks of Simon & Schuster, Inc. Beyond Words Publishing is a division of Simon & Schuster, Inc.

For more information about special discounts for bulk purchases, please contact Simon & Schuster Special Sales at 1-866-506-1949 or business@simonandschuster.com.

The Simon & Schuster Speakers Bureau can bring authors to your live event. For more information or to book an event, contact the Simon & Schuster Speakers Bureau at 1-866-248-3049 or visit our website at www.simonspeakers.com.

Manufactured in the United States of America

10 9 8 7 6 5 4 3 2

Library of Congress Cataloging-in-Publication Data

LeMay, Kathy.
   The generosity plan : sharing your time, treasure, and talent to shape the world / Kathy LeMay.
      p.   cm.
   Includes bibliographical references.
   1. Charities.   2. Humanitarian assistance.   3. Humanitarianism.   4. Social action.
5. Social service.   I. Title.

HV48.L46   2010
361.7'4—dc22

2009036685

ISBN 978-1-58270-234-6
ISBN 978-1-4391-5619-3 (ebook)

The corporate mission of Beyond Words Publishing, Inc.: *Inspire to Integrity*

Contents

To you, and the possibilities
you will unleash in the world.

Acknowledgments

You know that notion of it taking a village? That is most definitely true in the case of this book. This book would not have been possible without the generosity of my own personal village.

My family: Mom, Rick, Karen, and Trish. When it comes to who you are in the world and who you are to me, I am rendered speechless. I can only hope that these two words will suffice: thank you.

To my animals: thank you for ongoing joy.

I extend a lifetime of gratitude to Jacki Hoffman-Zehner, Barbara Dobkin, Anne Delaney, Molly Kreuzman, Shalini Kantayya, Katharine Ragsdale, Ayesha Mattu, Jensine Larsen, Emilia Stoneham, Mary Alex, Melanie Schnoll-Begun, Nancy Fellinger, Claudia Kahn, Michelle Drake, Lisa Tener, Shane Hammond, Anne Weiss, Ava Grace, and Amanda Weisenthal. Your contributions of time and talents toward the making of this book, together with your love and friendship, is more than I deserve, but I'll take it.

To my agent, Jeanne Fredericks, for your brilliant knowledge of publishing. Thanks for teaching me what I didn't know I didn't know. Thank you also for your kindness and commitment to this project.

Acknowledgments

Thanks to each of you who shared your generosity story and plan to help build this book. For privacy reasons, some names have been changed.

If this book is successful it will only be because the good folks at Beyond Words Publishing helped transform a training program into a manuscript—a very special thanks to Marie Hix and Cynthia Black. It's my privilege to know you and a gift to work with you.

Thank you to Pat Jenkins, for being my guide.

Lastly, to Michelle: thank you for making my world make sense.

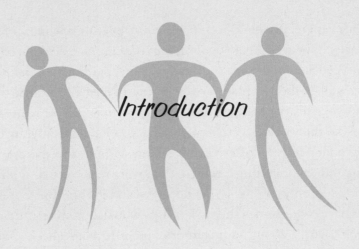

Introduction

When you hear the word *philanthropy*, what image comes to mind? For many, there's an immediate mental picture of people who are older, richer, and have lots of free time on their hands. There are people who write checks with no awareness of the number of zeroes, who spend afternoons at charitable board meetings and evenings at black-tie fundraising galas, or maybe people who travel around the world visiting war survivors, funding orphanages, or lending their esteemed names to important causes. These are positive associations—positive, but distant: people like Bill and Melinda Gates, Oprah Winfrey, the Buffet family. Big names, big causes, big wallets.

We often have differing associations with the idea of sharing wealth, yet the word *philanthropy* derives from the Greek word *philanthropos*, which means "humanity, benevolence, or loving of humankind." You'll notice the definition is not "loving of humankind … by contributing $1 million." Philanthropy is you and me doing what we can, with what we have, where we are, to borrow President Theodore Roosevelt's philosophy. Philanthropy is taking action for the greater good. Philanthropy is each of us contributing our time, our talents, and our financial resources to make a difference.

Chances are, you have been practicing philanthropy most of your life. If you have ever put a donation into the church collection basket, volunteered at a food bank or nursing home, participated in a fund-raising walk-a-thon or road race, or written a check to a cause that is near to your heart, then you are a philanthropist. If your intention is to make the world a better place, and you have given your time, opened your wallet, or offered your talents without an expectation of making money or getting a return, then you are a practicing philan-thropist. The only difference between you and me and Bill Gates: his checks have more zeroes and he has staff who help him create a plan.

Don't worry about adding more zeroes to your check; philan-thropy is not about how much. Philanthropy is intention combined with focus and action. What makes a difference in one person's life or in hundreds of lives is not merely a stack of checks; what makes a difference is you contributing your many gifts at your level and your capacity. *The Generosity Plan* will help you make the most of what you have to offer. It will not ask you to contribute more than you can, rather to contribute in a way that works for you and your life and, in doing so, benefits the causes you care about most.

There's no single dollar amount, no particular activity or cause that is better than another, no income level or demographic that matters to generosity, no set variable that is best for giving one's self to another in time of need. It's about finding your passion, envision-ing a better world, and putting yourself on the path to making that vision become a reality.

To help you get there, consider this book as your very own Generosity Plan staff. Inside you'll find tools, tips, and strategies for success. You will read about women and men just like you who have created plans that are changing the world for the better. You will find motivation, inspiration, and easy ways to make a difference. You will learn how to integrate philanthropy and the practice of giving into your daily life.

Starting today, you have the opportunity to build on your good works and your hopes for the future through creating a plan that will benefit the causes most important to you.

My Story

I grew up in New England, where my family and I lived a few different lives. We began in Connecticut: me, my two sisters, my mom and dad. A few years later, after my parents' divorce, it was just the ladies in Massachusetts. Those years—with just the four of us—offered their share of challenges, one of which was financial. My mother, like many great mothers throughout the world, sacrificed much to keep us going and to see us smile. She always worked and yet spent lots of time with us. She brought us to the public library and opened up new worlds. She taught us that one of our jobs was to help those in need. To this day, I still hope to become as good a human being as my mother. Plus, she's funny and fearless. (For example, during the George W. Bush administration, she sent him emails. A lot of emails. She shared with him how he had violated the Constitution and what he could have done instead. She is a fierce defender of democracy and, hands down, my greatest role model.)

When I was six years old, my mom married my stepdad. For a few years we were financially okay. We weren't the Rockefellers, but the bills got paid and for a short time we felt stable.

However, within a year of my mother's second marriage, my stepdad had to undergo multiple back surgeries, which eventually landed him on disability. Two years after, my biological father died of an inoperable brain tumor.

Throughout my childhood, finances were either okay, hard to come by, or downright scarce. Never were they abundant. For those of you who remember the Reagan administration and the era in the United States when cash was king, not having cash—living paycheck to paycheck—gives one a sense of not being good enough, of having some fatal flaw. Standing in the lunch line and paying with a reduced lunch ticket, getting free milk, visiting food banks—this was meant to feel shameful. But I don't remember if I felt ashamed. I remember feeling emotionally small because as a recipient, I felt as though I wasn't supposed to take up a lot space. This was a tough balance to strike since, despite living in meager accommodations, I felt powerful and passionate inside, as though my hopes and ideas could fill up mansions and estates.

And though there seemed to be whispers about those who received state aid, I was never ashamed of my family. I thought we were quite extraordinary. My mom was smart, funny the way Finns are funny, perceptive, hardworking, and equipped with an enormous capacity to laugh at herself and to love. My stepfather was the consummate storyteller. He would sit at our small kitchen table and, while drinking endless coffee and smoking too many unfiltered Camel cigarettes, tell us stories about ordinary happenings that made me feel as though we had traveled halfway around the world and back in under an hour. My mom and stepdad worked hard, and still, finances were rough. But, like so many others, we did the best we could. Life wasn't always rosy, but it was ours.

It was confusing then and painful to hear not-so-great things about what was termed the *working poor*. These days, there is less disdain for working poor people. When I was growing up, we were one of the scapegoats for troubles in the U.S. economy. Listening to the messages from government officials and people in high finance, I felt like I was draining my own country, not adding to her greatness, because we didn't have leisure money to spend.

At the same time, I felt I was smart and insightful and that I had huge gifts to offer. Plus, lots of things pissed me off. Inequality, apartheid, factory farms, child abuse, homelessness. I didn't have money, but I could stuff envelopes, write my congressperson, and sign petitions. And I did. Activism became the venue for my passion. I cared about a lot of causes and wanted to do my part. Though I didn't have a bank account, I had drive and, thanks to my Finnish ancestors, steel-hard determination.

As I got older, I read about people who made large gifts to hospitals, museums, libraries. They seemed to have fortunes, and I envied them a bit. Growing up in the working class of a small mill town, I longed for bigger and better things. I deeply believed that in order to make bigger and better things happen, you had to have money—and lots of it.

When I thought about this world of high-class people whose photos adorned society pages, it seemed far away from me. I imagined all sorts of different things. From my small-town vantage point, philanthropists were larger than life. They lived grand lives, like the women and men on the 1980s television shows *Dynasty* and *Knots Landing*. On shows like these, I saw huge, sprawling estates with wineries, staff who tended to the horses and washed the linens, and gorgeous, perfectly dressed women and men. These couples were giants of industries who made multimillion-dollar deals over lunch. They moved and shook the world. They manufactured automobiles, jets, ocean liners, and skyscrapers. And they gave back.

Their money erected new wings on hospitals. They cut long yellow ribbons at the sites of new day care centers. They christened the QE2 with expensive bottles of imported champagne. Their peers honored them at extravagant events. Impressive people gave speeches about them ("If it hadn't been for Jim and Margaret..."). From my vantage point, they seemed to have inherited the vocation known as philanthropy. They referred to themselves as fortunate and felt they should give back; it was part of their heritage. They, in short, were philanthropists.

I wanted to be that. I wanted that kind of money to give away. The image felt important and big: you were *seen* when you were that wealthy; doors opened for you; people considered your ideas. They may not always love those ideas, it seemed, but you were in newspapers, talked about on television. You got a seat at the table.

I saw myself at a larger-than-life oak desk signing checks while I talked to important people on speakerphone. *Imagine what I could do with that money!* I thought. As I lay on my twin-size mattress with my Kmart quilt draped over me, you should have seen the headlines that my funding made possible: "Animals Freed from Zoos, Returned to Their Protected Lands" and "Women's Human Rights Unleashed Throughout the Globe."

These fantasies fueled and overwhelmed me. I remained hopeful that I could make a difference, that my contributions would matter. At the same time, I felt daunted by the world's many problems. I felt small and unseen. I felt uncertain that I would ever amass the money one seemed to need to change the world. Weren't the world's great changemakers those people with a certain birthright or at least a certain size bank account?

On hot summer nights too humid for sleeping, I ran possibilities through my head. First things first: how exactly would I be able to change the world? I had two columns running in my head. The first: what mattered most to me. The second: what I needed to make a difference. I started a mental checklist:

- Angry about apartheid, the minimum wage, and homelessness?
  Check
- Own a sprawling estate?
  Ah ... no check
- Certain that I have the heart to help change the world?
  Check
- Been invited lately or ever to a ball that required me to take the jewelry out of the safe behind the fake painting?
  No check

Clearly I lacked money. Therefore, I would need to make as much money as I could. Here's what foiled that plan: I didn't seem to want any of the jobs that would actually make me philanthropist-size money. *How then*, I wondered, *can I ever be someone who can buy hundreds of books for children who have no books?*

Seeing no viable options for the big money, I felt overjoyed to learn the word *activist*. That, I could do. Lots of work with little pay. Right up my alley. I moved from volunteering to entry-level positions, then eventually to working as a fundraiser. Even then, when I was raising money and giving what I could, I still didn't identify as a donor. To me, writing $25, $50, and even $100 checks wasn't enough to say, "I am a philanthropist." Philanthropy still meant big money.

It wasn't until I turned thirty-one years old—after seventeen years of activism everywhere from Massachusetts to the former Yugoslavia—that I stepped in front of a crowd of four hundred at a philanthropy conference and, with my body shaking, named myself a philanthropist. The minute I said it, two women jumped from their chairs and cheered. And after my speech, six different women approached me and "came out" as blue-collar kids who were now in the field of philanthropy, trying to find their way. One woman said, "That speech was the permission I needed to make philanthropy my own."

Philanthropy is not about walking the road someone else has paved. If, starting today, the one thousand wealthiest people in the world gave away all their money, they still couldn't create a world that is just. They may provide capital to get things started, but it is our collective talents, resources, and passions that will hold, care for, and sustain community well-being. To state that philanthropy is for the affluent implies that only the most financially accomplished can create community. This is just not so. Those with vast resources do their part, and the rest of us need to do our part as well. The job will get done only when each of us gives of ourselves in the best and most powerful way we can. To get there, you must first see yourself as a powerful change agent. To give all you can, you can't think you aren't smart enough or good enough. You must know that you are the change you have been waiting for.

For me, identifying as a philanthropist required me to confront the very part of social change that I thought I could avoid: the topic of money. While trying to figure out if I loved money or hated it, I was fortunate enough to experience two defining moments while working for causes I cared about most. It was from these moments that the heart of philanthropy revealed itself to me: caring, compassionate people doing what they can, with what they have, where they are.

The Women of Bosnia, Herzegovina, and Croatia

In 1993, I was twenty-three years old and living in Seattle, Washington. I worked at a financial aid office and had just secured a researcher position—after relentless nagging and pursuing—with a professor at the University of Washington.

One morning, while walking to work, I passed by one of those outdoor magazine stands. Staring at me from the covers of *Time* and *Newsweek* magazines were two different photos of a similar and unforgettable image: Bosnian Muslim women wailing. The women's faces exhibited a horror I had never encountered. Of course, I knew about the siege in Bosnia and Herzegovina. I knew that women were being used as a tool for ethnic cleansing—I had studied women and war in college. But I hadn't seen their faces.

I frantically bought both magazines, hurried to work, sat at my desk, and read the brutal stories of rape-genocide camps in modern day Eastern Europe. I felt broken inside. It was as though someone had kicked me in the center of my body and knocked the wind out of me. I had of course read about past global atrocities like the Holocaust, but that preceded me. I wasn't alive during the Second World

War, but I had always asked: If they knew it was happening, why wasn't anything done about it? Why wasn't it stopped?

Now, here I was confronted with an atrocity that was current, happening right then. I felt overwhelmed. In the next few weeks, I got up every day, got ready for work, worked a full day, met up with friends for the movies, paid my bills, volunteered. I did my life, but I couldn't fully focus on it. I had nightmares about what these women were experiencing. I would close my eyes, and unthinkable images would pop into my head. But what could I do? I made $28,000 a year. I didn't know anyone with money. I didn't know anyone with power or influence. I didn't have Madeleine Albright's phone number, and President Bill Clinton wasn't waiting in the Oval Office for my call (although he should have been; he would have liked my suggestions).

Then came the opportunity. The professor I had spent months nagging to hire me told me that a friend of hers operated a refugee camp in the former Yugoslavia. She was going to volunteer at the end of the spring semester. Would I like to join her? I said yes.

I spent the next few months saving money and taking on extra work to earn enough to get to the Balkans. My girlfriend and I split dinners to save money. I got in touch with the women's organization I would be volunteering for. We sent faxes back and forth. "What can I bring?" I asked. "What do you need?" They needed infant formula, vitamins, and yarn for knitting clothes. Thanks to the goodness of others, I was able to fill suitcases full of donations.

Come August, I was ready to go. My professor friend called me to say she couldn't go after all. Something had come up with her husband's job, and he wouldn't be able to watch their three kids while she was away. I decided I would still go. So in September 2004, I boarded Air Croatia. There I sat on a tiny plane, with backpack in tow, surrounded by Yugoslavian businessmen on my way to a war-torn country.

The trip changed my life. I had the privilege of hiring a translator who brought me to refugee camps. There, I listened to stories of

men who had survived attempted massacres. I met a woman who, after being held prisoner for two months in a rape-genocide camp, walked from Sarajevo, Bosnia, to Zagreb, Croatia, with her two young children by her side. I met a woman with breast cancer who said, "I will deal with it later. Now, we must take care of our children." I helped to write appeal letters by women to the European Union and the United Nations. I sat in smoke-filled rooms while women survivors—most of whom had seen their husbands killed—talked politics and made plans for refugee care to ensure adequate shelter and food for the upcoming cold winter months. I went to a crumbling hotel and watched ten-year-old boys sit quietly, respectfully, and solemnly while women and men alike read poetry about survival.

And most of all, I learned that none of these good people were victims. I learned that these men and women, and most especially the women, would bear the burden of getting through an ongoing siege and do what it took to rebuild their country. They were poor, rural women turned family breadwinners; professional women transformed into fundraisers and shelter workers; and individuals who had become their country's rebuilders. They gave their time, treasure, talent, blood, sweat, and tears like nothing I had ever seen in my short life.

As I prepared to head home, I asked these women: "What can I do for you when I return to Washington State?" The women said, "Kathy, there are two things that we need. One, tell our stories so that no one forgets what we are going through. Two, we know what we need to do to get through this and to rebuild our lives, but we need resources to make that happen."

On the train ride to Austria en route to Germany, I felt my defining moment. Growing up, we lacked the resources to turn our hopes and ideas into the life we knew we wanted. Were it not for help along the way—reduced lunch programs, welfare support,

scholarships—I definitely would not be where I am today. Being a hard worker and tenacious is not all there is to the recipe for possibility. You need a support system, a safety net, and the tools to turn your hard work and tenacity into results.

Like my sisters and me, albeit on a different scale and in vastly different circumstances, the women and children of Bosnia and Herzegovina needed resources and a system to help them survive and, hopefully one day, thrive. I knew then that I would have to learn how to raise big money really well. My job, it appeared, would be to move money around so that everyone would have a fair and equal chance.

When I returned, I began volunteering with women who had also been to the former Yugoslavia. They had a nonprofit organization in place, and they took no salary. This was a labor of love. I was honored that they invited me to be a part of their efforts. We raised some money from foundations, but the bulk of the money came from individuals who bought T-shirts that had been donated to the organization. Twenty-five dollars at a time, we collected enough money to help children receive medical and psychiatric care, and we sent women who survived the rape-genocide camps to testify in front of the International Criminal Tribunal at The Hague, Netherlands.

I will never forget receiving the postcards of the women who had bravely traveled to The Hague to testify about their experiences. The postcards read, *We're here!* and *We made it*. One letter I recall stated, *I've testified. Now they can never say it didn't happen to us.*

What allowed these women to tell their stories that will forever be part of permanent records were not wealthy people writing $1 million checks. What enabled these brave women to become part of history were individuals from around the world—New Zealand, South Africa, Germany, the Netherlands, Indonesia, the United States—buying $25 T-shirts and writing notes on the order forms like: *Thank you for allowing me to help. . . . I didn't know what to do, and this has given me a small way to make a difference.*

What I learned is that each of us matters in another person's life as long as we take a small action. The women of Bosnia and Herzegovina were overwhelmed by how many women and men wrote checks to enable them to testify and receive care and treatment for themselves and their children. And although I didn't name it at the time, somewhere I knew that this was philanthropy in action for the greater good.

While the Bosnian and Herzegovinian women and those individuals who purchased T-shirts were my first defining moment, the second came shortly after. Since I volunteered for the organization supporting women in Bosnia and Herzegovina, I needed a job to pay for life and bills. I was fortunate enough to be hired as a fundraiser for an AIDS service organization, where I learned the ropes. I learned about event production, grant writing, and major gifts fundraising. I sent customized thank-you letters to our donors who gave $500 or more. I sat in on meetings where the conference table was covered in Excel spreadsheets and board members discussed who should approach donors x, y, and z and for how much. I knew my job was to be the support system for these fundraising volunteers. Mostly, I felt relieved that I didn't have to go out on "the asks"—an intimidating and anxiety-inducing task. I was happy to be behind the scenes.

Then one day, my colleague printed a report of donors who had made financial contributions for five consecutive years. He shared it with me. "Look at this," he said, handing me the database report. I looked at the record of a donor who had been giving consistently, every month, for more than five years. Her monthly gift amount: $5.

"Who is she?" I asked.

"I don't know. She lives in Texas, and we get a $5 check from her every month."

We checked her file, only to realize that the computer spit out the same thank-you letter to her each month. Because her one-time gift wasn't $500 or more, her letter was never customized with a personal note.

We stared at her record.

"I wonder what her story is."

My colleague said, "Maybe you should call her."

When you're a professional fundraiser, you often don't spend as much time discussing $5 or $25 donors as you do $10,000, $50,000, or $1 million donors (unless your organization is made up primarily of those smaller donors and they are the heart of your fundraising program). Rarely do committees form to discuss who should approach the donor who's been giving $50 per month in a two-year pledge program.

It's not that nonprofits don't see these smaller-money donors as critical to making a difference. They do. It's that there is a limited amount of time and human resources. To meet their mission, nonprofits need to be smart and strategic. This usually translates into meeting with those individuals who contribute big gifts.

Even though I didn't love this giving system, I lived it. It was my job. The problem? In doing so, I found myself implicitly stating to the $5-per-month donor and to donors like us all over the world, "We are not the ones who can have the maximum impact on the mission."

That day, I took my colleague's advice and called the $5 donor from Texas. Her story, the stories of the women I had met and worked with in the former Yugoslavia, and the countless stories I heard in the next seven years would transform how I conceptualized philanthropy. This woman was my second defining moment.

In the late 1980s, this donor's son was diagnosed with AIDS, but their hometown in Texas had no comprehensive services for people living with HIV/AIDS. Then her son heard about a nonprofit in Seattle that provided services for such people. He left Texas and moved to Seattle.

"I let him go," she said to me. "I knew I would never see my son again, but I couldn't help him. You could."

He called her when he got to Seattle, sent her postcards. He told her about getting food, home chore support, and rides to doctor appointments from an AIDS service organization. Shortly after, a staff member from the organization called to say her son had died, but he had not been alone.

"After that, I started sending your group all the extra money I have every month. I will keep sending you this until I am gone. I want to help other mothers' sons."

Years later, I met a woman with inherited wealth. This was an extraordinary donor who funded countless important projects throughout the United States and the world. From her own personal wealth, she had contributed more than $10 million to help those in need. She was a smart, seasoned, extraordinary woman from whom I learned so much.

I imagined that she must have felt powerful and that she had the tools she needed to make a difference. Living in this assumption, I once asked her, "How great does it feel to write a check for $1 million and know how much impact you are going to have?"

Here's what she said to me: "It's not like after writing a big check I go to bed and think, 'That's done!' I am a wreck that I can't do more. What good is all of this money if I can't just use it to create that magic wand?"

It hadn't ever dawned on me that a multimillionaire would feel that she had not done enough. That day, she taught me a marvelous lesson: philanthropy belongs to all of us because the world needs all of us to participate.

Here lived two different women. Two different checkbooks. Two different capacities. Each with a desire to help, to make a difference, to ease someone's burden or suffering. Each doing what she can, with what she has, where she is.

They, together, are the magic wand.

This work—making a difference, creating a better world—requires and depends upon each of us. All around the United States and the world, extraordinary acts of philanthropy are being performed every day. As the poet June Jordan so beautifully reminded us, "we are the ones we have been waiting for."

Jacki

When Jacki first created her Generosity Plan, she did so to be as effective as she could in her giving. "Spending time creating a Generosity Plan made infinite sense to me. When you think about it, we create financial plans, retirement plans, estate plans, emergency plans, health plans—why would you *not* make a plan for how you and your family are going to try to make the world a better place? Committing to the process and adding structure to the decisions on how to spend your time and your money is so empowering. Not only did I find I used both more effectively, but the result was a greater sense of joy from doing it. Having a Generosity Plan provides you with a framework that can include everyone in your family. Identifying your areas of passions and envisioning outcomes leads you to a set of actions. That is the essence of any plan. With this plan I truly feel like a Wonder Woman, and my family, the Incredibles!"

Your Generosity Plan can do the same for you as it did for Jacki. Your plan will help you make the world a better place by providing you with a framework for harnessing your passions and contributing your time, talents, and financial resources.

To be as effective as possible, you must first embrace these two key concepts: practicing generosity and making a plan.

Generosity is quite simply the habit of giving.

As a fundraiser, I have heard the word *generosity* used often, as in "He's a very generous man," or "She's done well for herself and is quite generous." In my field, *generous* is often code for "gave lots of money." It is the polite way to refer to people with resources versus saying, "He's loaded and gives away lots and lots of money."

Given that generosity is the habit of giving and not—as I previously assumed—having significant disposable income and writing big checks, I wondered how the two had become so closely linked. When I talked to folks with modest resources about being generous, they would most times refer to someone who had given their time when they didn't need to, or someone who had made a sacrifice for someone else's benefit.

Why, then, the strong links between generosity and big money?

The University of Notre Dame is researching the "genesis, manifestations, and benefits" of generosity. To better understand generosity in the present, they first looked back at notions of generosity in the English language. According to the university's science of generosity department: "Most recorded English uses of the word *generous* up to and during the sixteenth century reflect an aristocratic sense of being of noble lineage or high birth. To be generous was literally a way of saying "to belong to nobility."[1]

During the seventeenth century, however, the meaning and use of the word began to change. *Generosity* came increasingly to identify not literal family heritage but a nobility of spirit, with various admirable qualities that could now vary from person to person, depending not on family history but on whether a person actually possessed the qualities.

Generosity is truly about the spirit with which you approach making a difference. To make the most of your gifts, you must lead with a generous heart and a generous spirit. What does it mean to lead with generosity? While *generosity* is "the habit of giving," my definition of *leading with generosity* is the "habit of giving—especially when it feels out of your comfort zone, a little nerve-wracking, or downright terrifying." It is when you break through trepidations that you see in yourself all that you are truly capable of. When you play it safe—and we all know when we are playing it safe—you rob yourself of the chance to feel deeply fulfilled by your giving.

When, on the other hand, you envision all that is possible and match your giving to that vision, you are leading with generosity. To create the you that's possible, to unleash your inner change agent, you must practice generosity every day. As you think more about what being generous means to you and you work to complete the exercises in this book, you will see the generosity opportunities that present themselves to you daily. This book will help you transform your desire to be as generous as you can be into a Generosity Plan. With your Generosity Plan you will transform *generosity* from a noun to a verb. You will be giving at a level that is comfortable for you while reflecting your greatest generosity potential. You will become noble in spirit.

Generosity is magical. Think back to the first time you remember seeing someone behave generously. What was this first generous act you witnessed? What impact did it have on you in the moment? In your growth as a person? Do you carry that moment with you today?

When generosity is practiced, it allows us to beat the odds and create deep possibility in the world. When generosity is transformed from an occasional activity to a habit, a practice, a stretch, then the world lives its potential. Be as generous as you can be, in any way that you can be, in every moment that presents itself.

Being generous does not mean making a charitable gift that you cannot afford. However, being generous does mean writing any size check, even if you're worried about money.

Being generous does not mean overextending yourself to a point of fatigue and burnout. However, being generous does mean revisiting the priorities you set and ensuring that the material does not supersede the spiritual.

Being generous does not mean allowing others to take advantage of your talents and gifts. However, being generous does mean offering your talents and gifts without expectation of return.

We cannot ask of our business and political leaders to do that which we do not practice and model. Someone has got to illustrate what generosity and giving look like. As of this moment, that someone is you. By embracing generosity as a practice and a daily action, you will develop a habit of giving that will transform you and expand philanthropy to its fullest potential.

Developing a habit of giving is as vital as the process of developing a plan. A plan is required to make a real, lasting difference in the world. You can volunteer here or there, write checks in response to an annual request or a local fundraiser, or offer advice to a charity in need. However, when we are sporadic, it's difficult to gauge our progress, success, or impact. To really know you've made a difference—to see a change for the better—you must create a plan and work that plan. With generosity as your motivation, you will do more than you ever thought possible in service to those in need.

Today, you and I are going to transform philanthropy from meaning big wallets and big checks to meaning each of us doing what we can, with what we have, where we are.

I am giving you permission to let go of worrying about what you feel you cannot do or do not have: *If only I had a million dollars, I could really help* or *I don't have any special skills. I'm just a* _____ _____.

Instead of going to the negative, take today to open yourself up to your own unique generosity potential. Focus on unleashing your unique gifts and talents; imagine what you can do. Allow generosity to guide and transform you. Any one of us can recognize the power we have to make a difference. Once we know we want to give back to our fullest capacity, we then move into envisioning how.

How, then, do you get started? Here is one woman's journey toward living philanthropically and generously.

Robin

I met Robin through a mutual friend. Robin had just graduated from college, secured an administrative job in a financial services firm (hoping to eventually get her MBA and become a professional adviser), and was looking to meet women who were living their passion in their work.

Over iced tea in an outdoor café on a piping hot New England day, I learned about Robin's professional and personal goals. She enthusiastically shared her hopes and dreams for the coming years. Listening to her talk, I couldn't contain my ear-to-ear grin. Here lived a smart, caring, compassionate, hard-working woman who was ready to create an extraordinary life. "I love the idea of helping people create financial well-being for themselves. I hope that I can help them realize their dreams," she said.

When I asked her about her dreams, she said, "Of course to be with this firm for a while. And I would also like to have my own business one day—you know, go out on my own. Oh, and to travel the world. I want to make sure that girls everywhere have a chance at education. 'Course, to do that, I'll have to be some kind of billionaire, but maybe when I'm really old I can do that."

As our iced tea glasses were refilled, I didn't ask Robin how she defined *really old*. As someone nearly twenty years her senior, I imagined she meant one hundred and twenty instead.

I loved her ideas and her dreams, so I asked what she thought of starting her charitable and philanthropic work now.

"I wouldn't know where to start. Plus, I don't have any money, and I don't really know anyone yet."

I said, "I know that feeling completely. In fact, when I was your age, I thought the exact same thing. I've learned something pretty interesting in my past fifteen years of professional and activist work. I realized that I became a philanthropist not when I wrote my first big check, but when I was a kid in my mill town collecting coins for UNICEF at Halloween. The folks who gave me coins? They were philanthropists, too."

Robin looked at me with a combination of intrigue, a hint of *Oh no, my lunch companion might be crazy*, and a glimmer of hope.

I then shared with Robin what you will find in this book.

After that lunch and a few subsequent talks, Robin emailed me in the late fall. Her note said simply, "I got it. I am a philanthropist. There's no time to lose."

This book encompasses the collective wisdom of the literally thousands of people I have worked with and met who, like you, want to make the world a better place. They are what I came to call "unlikely philanthropists." They aren't billionaires. Their cell phone address books don't include heads of state. Yet they are transforming the world and, in doing so, transforming themselves.

The practices of these individuals are the practices you will learn here. This book will help you uncover your passion, unleash your hope, and develop concrete and achievable steps to help you make a difference.

If you're a soccer mom with three kids and little time to spare, you'll learn how to be a role model of philanthropy and generosity for your family and connect to charitable work that brings even greater gifts to your household. If you're a young professional working to build a strong career track, you'll learn how philanthropy can help you carve out a unique niche in your working life in a positive and powerful way. If you're nearing retirement and feeling the pressure to finalize your legacy, you'll learn how to ensure that your money and your values are in full alignment and how contributions of your time and talents now can make a difference today. If you're a business owner or self-employed and living with the pressures of managing your work 24/7, you'll learn how to manage your personal giving versus your small business's giving and how to engage your employees or interns in giving back.

No matter who you are, where you live, or how you define generosity—*generosidad, generosità, Großzügigkeit, gavmildhet, generosidade,* 慷慨—you can transform your generous spirit into actions that can change the world.

What Do Philanthropy and Generosity Look Like?

- African-Americans building churches and universities just one hundred years after being brought to the United States as slaves
- A small, quiet community exposing the dangers of a power plant and each community member giving time, talent, and treasure to make a difference
- Women in post-genocide Rwanda pooling their dollars to buy school uniforms for their children, generators for their villages, and bulk food to benefit the greater good
- Neighbors helping a man who might lose his home from a sub-prime housing loan
- The Cherokee Nation donating $3 million to the Oklahoma school system
- The Korean parent organization donating books and money to a library to ensure that students have the texts they need

- A community coming together to make sure that a neighbor's sick child can afford medical care and treatment
- Victims of the May 2008 earthquake in Sichuan, China, who, within hours of learning of loved ones' deaths, began handing out bottles of water to journalists to support their role in telling the story of the quake's devastation
- You giving "what you can, with what you have, where you are in support of the cause you care most about"

In Mexico City, I met a woman who made five pesos a day sweeping streets. She donated one of every five pesos to an orphanage. "They have less than me," she said. Would anyone say she is less of a philanthropist, less generous than Bill Gates? She epitomizes generosity. For her, giving is a habit, a part of her daily life.

Like this woman, you have in you the spirit of philanthropy, giving, and generosity. Now you have the opportunity to create a plan for yourself, with your family, with friends, or with your church, synagogue, or mosque. You can build off your own personal, familial, or religious traditions and witness the power of ordinary people like us doing what we can, with what we have, where we are.

There are countless ways you can give back, and this book will help you explore and uncover them. How you will give back may not seem obvious at first, but the more you practice generosity and commit to a plan, the clearer your contributions will become.

Michelle

At first, Michelle wasn't sure how she could contribute. As a working artist, she made her money from art sales and commissions. She booked photo shoots for weddings and bar mitzvahs. She also waited tables, managed cafés, and did administrative work. She was upset by the problems in the world but wondered what she could do to help.

"Most months I just barely pay my rent and living expenses. Maybe I have $5 or $10 left over, but what good will that do?"

Michelle could only see what she didn't have. Through working the exercises in this book, she was able to uncover the unique talents she could bring to helping those in need. "As I created a Generosity Plan, I realized that giving isn't all about money. Once I got past that hurdle, I focused on what I do have: talent as an artist, skills as an art teacher, and a belief that art can help and heal."

Within a few weeks, Michelle found a local organization that was looking to start an art program to benefit its clients. They were seeking artists who would teach art to and paint with adults with developmental disabilities. Michelle signed on right away. Five months later, Michelle and her student, Steven, took center stage at the organization's annual fundraising event. The experience transformed them, as people and as artists. Today, she and Steven continue to paint together, learn together, and share together. Their story inspired many in her community to donate their financial resources to the organization.

By focusing on what she could do, what she had to offer, Michelle ended up raising more money for the organization than she herself could have given—without even trying! She put aside focusing on what she couldn't do and instead allowed generosity, heart, and connection to guide her plan. Inspired by the work and moved by her own capacity to help, she planned to host summer painting events for adults of all ages, backgrounds, and disabilities.

With this book, you, like Michelle, will uncover your greatest gifts and talents. You will learn how to focus your talents and time for maximum impact. If you've never written a check or made a donation, you will feel the power of making your first charitable contribution that fully aligns your money and your values. If you have written a check, or many checks, but wondered if you've made a difference, you will learn to more effectively target your financial resources. If you've never volunteered because you weren't sure where to start, you will find the exact right volunteer commitment for you and/or your family. If you've been volunteering, but no longer feel inspired by how you're using your time, you will reconnect with volunteering in a way that best suits your personality and interests.

The Generosity Plan won't tell you the secrets to achieving a million-dollar career or give you anything you don't already have inside yourself. What this book *will* do is give you the exercises, tools, resources, and support you need to create a better world.

Now is the time for you to step into your philanthropic and generosity potential. The world needs what you have to offer. In fact, I don't think we can create the world we know is possible without every one of us doing our part. Today is the day we stop waiting for the big wallets to solve our world's problems. Today is the day we no longer ask what are *they* doing about hunger, poverty, a cure for cancer? Today is the day we realize we are the *they* we have always been seeking.

1
Getting Started
Going Back to Your Giving Roots

*A*t the heart of getting started on your Generosity Plan is going back to your giving roots. Each of us has roots in giving, be they based in culture, faith, personal belief systems, or family. These giving roots are a powerful force and have likely shaped your values and thinking today. By remembering these roots and recalling specific examples of how you or your family gave back, you will draw on traditions that will energize your present work and serve as the heart of your Generosity Plan.

If you've heard the phrase "You can't know where you're going until you know where you've been" and you agree with that belief, you are already well on your way to the getting started portion of your Generosity Plan.

Much like tracing ancestry, reconnecting with your giving traditions creates continuity in your philanthropic efforts. You will remember what you loved about making a difference. You will recall the good feelings that came with knowing you were doing something that helped someone in need. You will remember the part of you that gave without expectation of return. You will reconnect to being fulfilled by what you could do rather than worrying about what you couldn't do. You will likely uncover that you were involved in charitable work far earlier in your life than you initially thought.

Questions to Guide You

- What do I remember about giving in my family? Did my parents or guardians volunteer? Did we talk about those in need?
- Did my family encourage giving back? In what way? Through faith-based activities, school, community groups?
- What were the attitudes about giving back? Positive? Negative? Neither?
- Who did I see volunteering or helping out? What was a time when I or someone I knew helped a person or an animal in need? What feelings emerge when I describe the situation?
- Did I volunteer? If yes, when was the first time? Was I nudged to do it by a parent or teacher? How did I feel about it? How do I feel about it now?

Use these questions as a starting point, but don't let them limit your thinking. Write down your thoughts or share them with someone close to you. Ask a family member or friend to ask you questions about your giving. This will stimulate your thinking.

You may even experience a few *aha* moments that can dramatically impact your present and future course as well as how you see yourself as an agent of change. And, most important, you will reconnect with those activities that brought most meaning to your life. This happened for my sister, Tricia, when she went back to her giving roots.

Tricia

Tricia has a career she loves: working for a talent recruitment company. Prior to entering this industry, she had a career in the animal care field. After high school, she got her associate's degree in animal science and worked as a veterinary technician for thirteen years.

Tricia loves animals. And though she loved her work as a veterinary technician, she also struggled with seeing animals suffer and pass away. Needing a break, she branched out into management in the human medical field. Then, after relocating, she landed her current position.

To stay connected to her passion and to make a difference in the lives of animals, she became a member of several animal protection groups. She was part of monthly pledge programs. She signed petitions. She voted for better conditions for racing dogs and farm animals. She forwarded action emails to friends and family. And while this had helped, it wasn't enough. Tricia didn't feel connected to the cause she cared about. She didn't feel fulfilled.

To discover what was missing and what more she could do, Tricia went back to her giving roots, to our family's giving traditions. In looking back, she discovered that as a child she felt most fulfilled being hands-on. As a kid, she would find a stray on the street, scoop it up, take it in, and find it a home. When it came to animals in need, Tricia became the go-to person in our family and in our neighborhood. She felt most herself when she was helping an animal that had no other advocate. Tricia came from a line of caretakers: our mother, who showed us what compassion looked like; our grandmother, who volunteered as a nurse during the war in Finland. My grandmother, my mother, and my sister: they're hands-on givers. They nurture. They provide care to those in need, one person / one animal at a time.

For Tricia, adding volunteering at a local animal shelter to her Generosity Plan made her strategy complete. "I went back to my roots and discovered that I am happiest and most fulfilled when I am there for animals who haven't yet been adopted. I know my time with them makes them more comfortable. For those few hours, they have a companion who will come back week after week. I hadn't realized what a gap it was for me. I'm glad to write checks and sign petitions; I know these efforts are important. Equally important is being there with the animals. It makes a difference in their quality of life and in mine."

By looking back, you will reconnect with the things that you did which were most fulfilling. You will access and recapture your own family's giving traditions. Draw on what fulfilled you; draw on your own or your family's giving traditions; draw on your roots. This practice will add continuity to your plan and help you connect past, present, and future.

Debi

Debi is a successful corporate executive. With multiple degrees and the smarts and savvy to know when to make tough decisions, she excels at her work. She loves her job. She is also grateful for the opportunity to give back. Debi serves on multiple nonprofit boards. She makes personal contributions to the organizations, gets her company to share some of its wealth with these causes, organizes events, and sells tables for fundraising events. All in all, Debi contributes a great deal to causes that are near and dear to her heart.

I was surprised then that she asked to meet with me to help her create a better giving plan. After she shared how she was contributing, I asked her what she thought was missing from her plan. She said she wasn't sure, but her giving seemed to lack *oomph!* "I should be more excited about what I'm doing, but really sometimes I feel like I'm just checking off my philanthropic to-do boxes. It feels more like my position at work than giving back."

So we went back.

Debi grew up in Brooklyn, New York, in the 1960s. Her parents were her anchors, providing her with a loving, albeit strict, home. In her home, Debi learned the value of working hard and giving back. And though she and her family didn't have money for travel, she told me about her father taking her "all over the world through books." Her father would say, "Reading is the key to personal freedom and liberation." Debi read books—a lot of books.

When her aunt got sick, her parents sent Debi to her aunt's apartment, just down the street, to read to her. What started as reading to her one time a week turned into two times, then three times. "I didn't really think about it, I just did it. She seemed to enjoy it so much. I couldn't imagine why listening to me read helped her, but it did, so I did it." Debi read to her aunt for months on end, until her aunt passed away. "I had gotten pretty used to our reading time. When she died, I missed her and I missed that time we had together. It was pretty special."

The years passed, and Debi graduated from high school, went on to college, and then attended graduate school for her master's degree in business administration. She volunteered a little, but she was focused on her career and on building a family.

She had reached her goals: husband, two beautiful daughters, successful career, leadership in the philanthropic community—but she felt something was missing. I asked her how fulfilled she was by serving on boards. She said she knew she was helping, but she felt removed from the charitable aspect. I asked her if she thought that reading to her aunt was her first philanthropic contribution. She smiled. "I guess I thought of philanthropy as something formal, something that happens in boardrooms. But you know, you're right. I loved helping my aunt."

I asked her what she thought about volunteering to read to the elderly. She smiled but then questioned it. "Well, I guess I thought that's what you did when you were younger and couldn't write checks or sit on boards. Then, as you got older and acquired skills, you moved away from that kind of work. I've seen myself in boardrooms for so long, I think I forgot that I could be with the people we're trying to help."

Like Tricia, Debi missed the hands-on giving she practiced when she was a girl: reading to her ailing aunt. But, when I pressed, she said it was her most fulfilling volunteer experience.

Simple acts become transformative acts. None of us outgrows hands-on helping, one-on-one support; those connections are what fuel us. Those interactions give us hope. Take the time to go back to when you made a difference—before you had a bank account, before you wondered how many zeroes to put on a check, before you wondered if you were qualified enough to volunteer. By going back, you will remember how good you felt, as those feelings are still a part of you. They can fuel and inform your generosity efforts today.

To help you with your going back, start a Generosity Journal. (Don't worry. You won't need to start journaling in a formal sense.) Think of it instead as a notebook where you jot down ideas, create outlines, record your thoughts. My own Generosity Journal is 8½" × 11" copy paper that was on its way to the recycling bin. Yours can be a bound journal, a notebook, or a pile of scrap paper. The most important part of the Generosity Journal is not what's on the outside but what's on the inside.

By keeping a journal, you will be sure to capture all those great *aha* moments that could have an important impact on your Generosity Plan. This happened for Chrissie, who learned she had been giving back and making a difference for a lot longer than she initially recalled.

Chrissie

When I first talked with Chrissie about her initial memory of making, or wanting to make, a difference, she recalled volunteering at a hospital when she was nineteen. She volunteered as a candy striper during her first year of college and said that the experience made her feel "like I was brightening people's days."

She continued, "What I remember about it is how such a little thing, like a magazine, a smile, a ginger ale refill, could make such a difference. That, and I was already really, really tall. I felt like I loomed over their beds! One patient called me Wonder Woman. I loved it."

Chrissie initiated her own volunteering—it wasn't part of a community service program or her degree. She wasn't majoring in medicine. She majored in the arts. Based on this, I had a feeling that she likely started giving back before she entered college. I asked her about it, and she replied, "No, I don't think so. Well, not anything of significance. I collected food for a food drive at school. I remember giving blood at a blood drive. Oh, and when we were kids, my mom had us make up homemade cards for the older people in church who had gotten sick."

I asked her why she thought she didn't tell me about these experiences when she initially talked about the first time she can remember giving back.

"I think I didn't recall those because I thought that was just what you did—helped when you could. Now that I've made money, I think I haven't seen volunteering as philanthropic. Talking with you, I realize how philanthropic my family was, in our way—in the way that we could be."

Looking back helped Chrissie realize that her family did indeed have a tradition of generosity. As she continued to create her Generosity Plan, she shared how this early exercise benefited her: "Before these exercises, I felt like an amateur. No one in my family had much money to give. When I made a decent enough salary to be able to write checks that got me handwritten thank-you notes, I felt like I was on my own. I didn't know how to 'do philanthropy.' I then realized that I did have a tradition of philanthropy in my family. I felt less alone and more equipped. Behind me were generations of parents and grandparents giving to their capacity. Giving to my capacity carried forward these traditions."

Looking back helped Chrissie reconnect to her giving roots, recall that she has always been a philanthropist, and increase her confidence as she moved forward. She also created new traditions of giving in her family, including involving her children in the giving money part of philanthropy. She wanted to ensure that her children appreciated the concepts of spending, saving, and sharing and didn't want them to go through the anxieties she experienced when she first started writing checks to her favorite causes.

What if you're married and have children? How can going back to your giving roots as a couple enrich your joint generosity experience? How can going back help to pass on to your children the best of their family roots?

Mark and Ellen

I met Ellen years ago through a mutual friend. She had left the high-paced world of finance and was ready to be as serious in her giving back as she had been in her professional work. Like Chrissie, Ellen felt that she didn't have solid philanthropic roots.

When she was growing up, her family had been lower-middle class. She hadn't seen her parents write checks or even talk about money. Now that she had made money of her own, she felt she needed a guide.

After a few coffee dates with Ellen, I met her husband, Mark. Mark had also made money in finance and was now pursuing a new vocation. They both felt they had been successful but that something was missing. I shared with them that my good friend York Mayo talked about retiring after a successful business career, waking up one morning, and realizing he was ready to go from "success to significance." This resonated with Ellen and Mark, who said that this was what they were seeking.

Ellen and Mark wanted to jump right into giving. They showed me a list of everyone they had written checks to and asked: Who should we remove? Who should we keep? How do we know when to say yes? When to say no? How do we know when to say yes to a larger gift request?

I then began with the exercise of going back to their giving roots. As Mark and Ellen focused on results and outcomes, they were wary about this exercise. "Neither of our families had money," they said. "How will this exercise help us give ours away?"

I shared with them that they very likely have seen charitable acts in their lives—acts that have had an impact on how they think about giving back. I shared that if they wanted to lead a life of significance, they must first look at what they thought was significant when they were growing up. What mattered to them? Who was a role model? Who wasn't a role model?

As we began the exercise, Ellen recalled her mother volunteering her time and donating canned goods to local charities. Mark remembered that his mother was also active, coordinating blood drives for the local hospital and donating books to the library. Neither Ellen nor Mark could specifically recall checks being written; if they were written, their mothers didn't share this portion of their giving with them. Similarly, neither remembers their fathers volunteering or writing checks.

What did this mean for them as they approached their Generosity Plan?

In their current family, Ellen had taken the lead with their family's giving: researching the charities, deciding a gift amount, and mailing in the checks. Both Ellen and Mark felt passionately about the same issues and causes, and both felt an obligation to give back to those who were not as fortunate. No doubt, these feelings originated from their familial roots. However, when it came down to thinking about which groups to write checks to, and for how much, or places where the family could volunteer as a whole family, Ellen bore the responsibility.

As we explored this more, Mark said to me, "I never thought before about why I left most of our foundation giving work to Ellen; I think I thought she was more organized than me. I realize now that I have always just thought women volunteer and host events at their home for a local charity. I show up and smile, and I certainly care about the cause, but I learned that it was something that women take care of."

This is not the first time I've heard this story. In fact, this may be true in your family's giving history or in your family structure today.

In Mark and Ellen's case, they asked themselves: even though this is how it was done in our households when we were growing up, does the same approach work for our family today? This one question helped them pose and resolve a new set of questions about the family's involvement in giving back. They asked themselves:

- Do we want to have our son and daughter seeing just Mom spearhead the giving and volunteering?
- For Mark: How much am I missing by being on the fringe and not really getting more involved in the work?
- For Ellen: I think that women do lead a lot of efforts in their household. However, the causes we care about will be much better served if the whole family gets deeply involved.

This shift in thinking from *Mom will do it* to *This is an effort for the whole family* brought them to the place of posing these questions:

- What are the most important causes to us as a family and to each of us individually?
- At what age should we begin to involve our children? When is too young? When is too late?
- Are we happy writing a check and getting updates in the mail, or do we want to meet with the group and get involved beyond the check?
- What inspires us most? What work do we see truly making a difference?
- How would we like to balance our giving (i.e., how much to our alma maters, to social service groups, to international organizations, and so on)?

Today, Ellen and Mark have a Generosity Plan that involves the whole family, and they both believe that taking the small amount of time to go back to their giving roots *before* moving forward helped them to become more thoughtful and intentional in their generosity activities. "We learned which [family] habits ... we wanted to reclaim, and we learned which habits wouldn't benefit us in moving forward. We feel we've created new giving traditions that involve our children."

From Tricia's, Debi's, Chrissie's, and Ellen and Mark's stories, you can see the power of accessing your roots and your family's traditions to remind yourself what you most love about giving back and to inform your present and future efforts.

What, though, should you do if you look back and see an absence of giving traditions, or see traditions that you'd rather leave in the past? What steps can you take if you don't have a giving history that can support your present and future Generosity Plan? What do you do if you don't feel connected to a family custom?

This very thing happened to Neil when he began looking back.

Neil

When I met Neil, he told me that he had no giving traditions from which he could draw inspiration. Born and raised in the Midwest in the 1950s, Neil felt lost when it came to figuring out the source of his generosity values.

"What's funny about my life, I come from what a lot of people would consider a privileged background. We never went without. My father was a good provider. My mother made sure we ate, had good clothes, and had a warm house. But my life growing up was a lot like those television movies you see: Dad works all day, makes a drink when he comes home, and sits in front of the television, aloof and distant. Mom scurries about, making sure Dad has what he needs and asking us kids to keep it down.

"Ours was not a house where you brought home candy bars for Dad to sell at work to help pay for gym equipment. Mom made sure we got off to school every day, and she greeted us when we got home. But Dad liked her home, so she didn't serve on the PTA like other moms."

For Neil, the exercise going back to his giving roots required that he look beyond his immediate, nuclear family for his role models. In his Generosity Journal, Neil answered the questions:

- Outside of your parents and siblings, who were your other relatives: grandparents, aunts, uncles, cousins? How often did you see them? Can you recall a relative who did something that inspired you?
- Was there a teacher or coach who inspired you? Did he/she go out of his/her way for you? What do you remember about that?
- Can you recall an act of kindness from someone in your immediate surroundings who made an impact on you? What was it? What did you feel about it?

As he answered these questions, Neil recalled a handful of instances that helped him to feel a connection to traditions greater than himself. In middle school, Neil was quiet and didn't fit in. He was a shy and average student. A math teacher approached Neil and told him he recognized talents in him. He gave him additional assignments and extra credit. Neil learned to love math, and he went on to take advanced level math in high school. In his journal he wrote, *I got absorbed in math. I don't think I ever thanked that teacher for what he did. I guess you could say he was just doing his job, but to me, it was someone who believed in me.*

This teacher's generous act helped Neil realize that working one-on-one with people who have been left out is what matters most to him. Though Neil's family did not possess obvious giving traditions, by digging a little deeper and expanding his view, he was able to see generosity practiced by others in his early years.

ᚎ

If you're like Neil, remember that you can uncover a role model you have met along the way. One simple act can help you recognize how you want to practice generosity today. This is true for all of us, even the forty-fourth president of the United States.

President Barack Hussein Obama

In October 2007, while campaigning in Iowa to become the next president of the United States, then-senator Barack Hussein Obama was asked by a man in the crowd, "What would you say is the most painful and character-building experience of your life that puts you in an important position to make important decisions of life and death and the well-being of our country?"

He replied:

I would say the fact that I grew up without a father in the home. What that meant was that I had to learn very early on to figure out what was important and what wasn't, [to] exercise my own judgment, and in some ways, to raise myself.

My mother was wonderful and was a foundation of love for me, but as a young man growing up, I didn't have a lot of role models and I made a lot of mistakes. But I learned to figure out that there are certain values that were important to me that I had to be true to.

Nobody was going to force me to be honest. Nobody was going to force me to work hard. Nobody was going to force me to have drive and ambition. Nobody was going to force me to have empathy for

14

other people. But if I really thought those values were important, I had to live them out.

That's why it's so important for me now ... to wake up every morning and ask myself, am I living up to those values that I say are important?

Each of us has the opportunity to wake up every morning and ask: What matters most to me? What one thing can I do today that will make a difference for someone I know or for someone I may never meet?

To ensure you uncover this passion in you and develop an intentional and thoughtful tradition of giving in your own life, here are three simple things you can do today:

1. **List three different acts of your own personal generosity.** Chances are very likely that you have given selflessly for the benefit of others. List three different times when you have given to someone without expectation of return. How did you feel when you gave of yourself? What was the impact on the recipient? What do those actions say about you and what you value?

2. **Make a list of individuals who inspire you.** Who inspires you? Have you read a story recently about someone whose actions were admirable? Who in the public eye do you look up to? Have you been inspired by a neighbor? A coworker? Whether you are inspired by the works of a great spiritual leader or by the efforts of someone you've met in passing, list the traits of that individual. Which of these traits do you want to continue to cultivate in you? How can your Generosity Plan support you in living those qualities?

3. **Create a Generosity Club.** Like book clubs, money clubs, or investment clubs, Generosity Clubs allow you to share your knowledge and benefit from others' experiences. The group environment can help you unleash your best thinking, take action, leverage efforts, and get ideas to support you in your generosity efforts. (For more on starting your own Generosity Club, see chapter 10.)

Going back to your giving roots, accessing your family's giving traditions, and creating the conditions for habitual generosity puts you firmly on the road to creating your Generosity Plan. Take the time now to go back, and it will serve you in the days, months, and years to come. You will know what you stand for and why you stand for it, and from this you will turn your hopes into realities.

2

If I Ran the World...

Unlocking Your Vision and Setting Your Priorities

*I*f going back to your giving roots is the heart of your Generosity Plan, then unlocking your vision is its soul. This step will accomplish multiple goals, guiding you to make the right charitable decisions by clarifying exactly what you care about most and what moves, motivates, and inspires you. By unlocking your personal vision, you will learn to lead and give from a place of hope and possibility rather than from a place of overwhelm or uncertainty. As a result, you will give your time and resources to only those causes about which you are most passionate. This approach will maximize your impact, and help you to make the difference you long for and are fully capable of making.

There are a handful of different definitions for *vision* or *vision statement*. My favorite is this one from the website timethoughts.com from author Rodger Constandse: "A vision statement is a vivid, idealized description of a desired outcome that inspires, energizes, and helps you create a mental picture of your target."

If you've heard people speak about vision statements, chances are you've heard about them in the corporate sector or at big private foundations. Vision statements are not just for big institutions with big money. They are for any businesses, organizations, families, or people who want to ensure that they know what they stand for and work for each day.

Unlocking your vision is key to your long-term success. So many times, I have seen people jump right in to giving without really defining their values, or passions, and then they find themselves giving at the office, sponsoring a walk-a-thon, buying cookies or candy bars for school groups without having a concrete reason for why they are doing it or what they are trying to create. Without a vision statement to guide you, you will end up all over the map, giving here, giving there, giving here and everywhere, and wondering if you are making any headway.

With a vivid and powerful description of the change you want to see, you put yourself on track toward transforming an idea into a reality. Making change requires focus; scattered won't do. Your vision statement will clearly identity your hopes, dreams, and passions.

Unlocking your vision can and should be a transformational experience for you. To help you create it, take some time to write in your Generosity Journal the responses that come up from these questions:

- What is wrong in the world?
- What is broken that needs to be fixed?
- What do I care about most in the world?
- What else matters to me?
- What keeps me up at night?
- What gets me out of bed in the morning?

When I first asked myself these questions, I was grateful for the structure they provided. I wanted to do everything. I wanted to be a part of every cause. So many efforts seemed worthwhile. How would I decide which areas I would choose to be a part of, to make a part of my life?

By answering these questions, I uncovered my deepest passions. I removed clutter from my brain and gave myself permission not to be the champion of all causes. By creating my own personal vision, I have also let go of feeling like I have to support all worthwhile endeavors. Instead, I focus on those problems in the world that keep me up at night. I told myself the truth about what matters most to me and what I could envision committing my life to. This doesn't mean that I won't expand my horizons as I grow older, but I will do so thoughtfully and with a plan.

The most powerful question I answered so many years back was: what keeps me up at night? I remember once crawling into bed very late. I had worked a twelve-hour day and was exhausted. Sitting on the nightstand by my bed was a stack of should-reads. You likely know what I mean. In the stack are magazines, journals, articles, a book or two weighing down the emails you've printed out and promised yourself you'd get to. Those many years ago, I had a particularly unruly stack. I decided I would take the advice of an organizational expert who said, "Only touch a piece of paper once." Whoops. I am certain I had touched each of these almost two dozen times thus far. Committed to getting more efficient, I pulled the stack from the nightstand to my bed and began to go through it, starting with the top piece of paper. Three papers into the stack, I was done for. I hadn't been interested in the first two but thought, *I should read these. I should know more about how the use of technology is creating better solar power and new therapies in treating Parkinson's disease.* Both of these areas are critically important. However, they aren't my passions.

I found myself touching the papers, journals, magazines, and books way more than once just to get to the topics I truly wanted to learn more about: strategies to empower women globally, what it means to build a movement, and what it will take to close down factory farms. These are my passions, my heart's work. When I identified them, I knew I was beginning my journey toward smartly contributing my time and talents to the world.

There is no right or wrong cause to get behind. While you may be impressed by someone's dedication to their cause, you needn't feel pressured to get involved in their work—unless that work is your calling. You have what matters to you, what you will learn about, what you will stay the course with. When you unlock your vision, you have accomplished a key component toward leading and living your generous life.

When Stephen asked and answered the questions about his greatest passions, he unlocked a new world of giving.

Stephen

As a seasoned philanthropist—his family had been involved in charitable giving for generations—Stephen wasn't sure how a vision statement would help him. He served on different nonprofit boards and wrote checks to several organizations, some of which were organizations his parents and grandparents had funded, while others were ones that friends and colleagues had asked him to support over the years.

When I met Stephen, he wasn't sure he needed a generosity coach. After hearing him talk about how much money he gave away and how much he volunteered, I wasn't sure he needed me either. Then we dug a little deeper.

For most of his life, Stephen had contributed his time and his financial resources to three different areas: the arts, music, and education.

I asked him why these causes were meaningful to him. He shared stories of having a great middle and high school education, one that helped develop his skills and talents even though he had never been the star student or athlete. About music and the arts, he said that he believed in organizations that had been around a long time. He spoke of feeling confident investing in organizations that had proven track records of success and stable financials while contributing to a wide range of people.

I then asked him what he thought was wrong in the world; what did he think was broken that should be fixed? Stephen was quiet, but only for a few seconds. His answer, based on what he had already said were his giving priorities, surprised me. Stephen said that what was wrong in the world was tyranny and dictatorships. He said he thought tyranny in any and all forms was wrong. I asked him why he felt it was wrong and what harm it caused.

He said that tyranny deprived individuals and communities of the opportunity to reach their fullest potential. It thrived when people suffered and went without, and nothing about a system like that could be right. As he spoke further, his eyes were lit up and he spoke about the need to make sure that tyrants never be allowed to rise to power. He spoke passionately and eloquently about how much more of an impact food aid and literacy programs would have if governments supported the well-being of all their people.

On that sunny morning on Stephen's deck, I took another bite of pastry and high-fived him. I then asked him how this vision, this hope for all the world's people, connected to the organizations he'd been funding. He paused, laughed, and said, "It doesn't. Why *am* I giving to these groups?"

As we explored further, he realized that the organizations he had supported were important to him and to his family's giving history. He would always want to give his time and his resources to them because these organizations were part of his family's giving roots.

For Stephen, unlocking his own personal vision for the world allowed him to expand upon his family's giving traditions, make his personal mark, and have a deep soul connection with his Generosity Plan.

He then wrote his vision statement, which read: *I believe in a world where every single person should have the same opportunities and the same access to learning, earning, music, and the arts. I believe that governments can work each day to serve the needs of their people and that real fairness begins when real democracy is practiced.*

Stephen's vision statement unlocked in him one of his greatest passions, which he had not before explored or funded. When I asked him why he thought he hadn't pursued this belief in democracy, he said that he felt a bit overwhelmed by it all and wondered how he could make a difference. As he completed the next steps of his Generosity Plan, he realized that he could and would have an impact in this area.

Vision statements serve us all, no matter our professional status, income level, or age, or how long we've been giving.

I share with you these two tips to create your vision statement and help it *pop*:

1. **Stand for something not against something.** If your deepest passion is an end to hunger, instead of saying, "My hope is to see hunger eliminated," write, "I envision a world where all people have an abundance of healthy, nutritious food that serves them in their daily life and in meeting their highest potential." Create a vision statement that is hopeful, positive, forward thinking, and that allows you to see possibility.

2. **Be specific.** Instead of saying, "I envision a world where everyone gets a good education," write, "I envision a world where we all make educating our children a top priority." Specificity asks you to dig a little deeper and learn about what you want to change and where you think that change should happen. For some, equality happens through legislation; for others, through education. Both viewpoints are correct, and both types of people need to find what motivates them into action.

Years ago, I read a story that I'll paraphrase for you now. Even though the story isn't about righting a wrong in society, it encompasses the power and possibilities in naming a huge vision, because you see something bigger than you, greater than you—something that can and should outlast and outlive you. The story is about the entrepreneur and automaker Henry Ford:

At a meeting of the Ford Motor Company board of trustees, Henry Ford named his vision: that someday every American will have a car in his garage. The trustees of the Ford Motor Company—likely a practical bunch—looked at Mr. Ford in disbelief. They told him that his statement was unrealistic and unachievable. They said it wasn't a smart business strategy and that the company would go broke trying to make such a thing happen. Henry Ford disagreed.

From Mr. Ford's vantage point, if you set a vision that you could achieve in your lifetime, it wasn't really a vision for the future; it was more of a goal. He said he certainly didn't expect that he or anyone in the room would live to see the day, but the vision had to be set in stone so that it would guide future company presidents, future trustees. He challenged his trustees by stating that if they only aim to sell a car to a percentage of Americans, then they wouldn't need to build more factories, employ more people. At one point, this goal will be hit. Then what? Mr. Ford asked his board to envision what could be—what might be someday. His board eventually acquiesced, and today, most

Americans—for better or for worse—have two cars in their garage. Not even Henry Ford could envision *two* cars in every garage. His vision was forward thinking at the time, and even so, the reality exceeded the vision.

We each must create a vision statement bigger than ourselves, then build a Generosity Plan that moves us one step closer to making that vision a reality. Henry Ford's vision for the Ford Motor Company "captured the imaginations of others, mobilized resources, and reshaped the reality of their times."[2]

How can your vision statement capture your imagination and propel you toward making the difference you are capable of making? Let your vision run free. Like Mr. Ford, you never know what it will create.

My friend Jacki did exactly this.

Jacki

When Jacki created her vision statement, she went big. She had always felt something inside of her, calling her to step up in a big way, but she hadn't really found the venue for these passions.

Born and raised in a small town in British Columbia, Jacki went to college in Vancouver to study business. After graduation, she moved to the United States to pursue a career on Wall Street. While she loved the fast-paced and high-intensity environment, she also longed to make a difference for women in the corporate world as well as for women around the globe.

Jacki is a Christian and values being in service to others. She believes that a just world is achieved when women and girls are respected and treated fairly, as equals to men and boys. She considers the equal treatment of women to be a cornerstone of Christianity, and she sees herself as a steward of this effort.

When she created her vision statement, Jacki had a lot of ideas to juggle. As a highly successful businesswoman, entrepreneur, mother, wife, blogger, networker, philanthropist, and community leader, she saw so many opportunities to make the world a better place. Jacki's vision statement—and her concept of generosity that drove her vision statement—helped her develop a sharp focus for her philanthropic efforts. Jacki's vision statement reads: My life's work is to help create a most just and equitable world for women and girls. I believe that it is through the education and empowerment of the one half of our population that the whole population will benefit. We need to move towards gender equity if we want to have a positive and sustainable future.

As she took the steps to live this vision statement, Jacki found that her vision and her commitment to generosity were becoming paramount in all parts of her life, not just in her philanthropy. Jacki shared that philanthropy and giving were a critical part. The more she invested in them, the more they became the driver in her life. She stated that her hopes for the future now help her make decisions about business and other endeavors.

When we started working together, Jacki could not have predicted how her big thinking would help to transform her present and future. About this, Jacki said, "My capacity to give has been expanded because now I see the hope and opportunity in everything I do, all the time, every day."

While creating your vision statement may not jump-start a new calling or career, you never know what it will unleash in you, and how it will, in turn, powerfully and positively impact the people and the causes you care about most.

In my years of creating Generosity Plans with great people like Stephen, Debi, Tricia, Jacki, and so many more, one of the early hurdles that emerges in the process of creating vision statements is the dreaded practicality. Practicality shows up in statements such as, "Well, not that this is ever going to happen, but …" or, "What I envision is *x*, but I can't imagine all the leaders getting behind this …" or even, "I hope for this, but I can't see how we can get out of the mess we're in to even get there."

When creating a vision, leave practicality at the door. Practicality—how to make the vision work—will emerge when the time is right. Practicality is a great tool that will help you *actualize* your vision, but it will not be useful in helping *create* your vision.

If, while creating your vision, you discover the practicality voices drowning out the vision voice, try one or both of these exercises. In no time, you will be knocking down the practicality hurdles left and right:

- Repeat this quote to yourself: "Every new idea looks crazy at first." Now, list ideas that were once thought to be crazy but have worked out pretty well—for example the concept that the Earth is round, the end of the seven-day workweek and the introduction of the weekend, American women voting.
- By yourself or with a small group, answer these two questions: If I ran the world, could I make the changes I wanted, and if there were no limitations, what three things would I implement starting today? These can be large or small. You may say, "Make sure every school has enough teachers, computers, and books so that no student goes without" or "Ensure that every single person has a job to go to and that there is another employment opportunity available if someone is laid off." The more you practice saying the big, hopeful, absurdly wonderful

statements, the closer you will get to landing on your passion and setting the course for your Generosity Plan.

As you think about what you would do if you were in charge, you may find yourself saying that you don't know exactly what you'd do, that you hadn't thought of it before, or that other people have been elected to answer this question. Few of us are ever asked our opinion about the state of the world and what we think will make it a better place. Most of us are bombarded with other people's ideas and messages. As a result, we tend to agree with one or disagree with another as we react to other people's ideas. Here is your chance to share your idea, your hope, and your vision. And later, as we move forward with your Generosity Plan, you'll then know which charitable groups are a match and which are not.

Take your time in unlocking your vision. Ask for help from people who support you. If you don't have an answer right away, no worries at all. Your mind is busy right now, working to remove the barriers to your vision. It takes a little time; there's no need to rush the process. What you can do, however, to move the process forward, is write. Write anything. Write the first thing that comes to mind. Then write the second thing that follows, and so on.

Remember that the place of vision and imagination is a place all your own. There are no deadlines and no kids who need protractors for tomorrow's geometry class. There is no rush hour, no heartburn from too much coffee. There are no bills to pay. There is no shortage of money. In your space of vision and imagination, no one goes without and there is enough for everyone. There is enough for you.

Spend some time reviewing what you wrote. Did it seem just about right? Were you surprised like Stephen was? When you read your vision, did you feel hopeful? Did you feel inspired? If you read this vision to others, how did they respond? If you imagine reading this vision to a young person, would you be proud of what you wrote?

For her vision to mean a lot to her, Jill imagined that someday her great-great-grandchildren might read it. She thought of them when she wrote it. I was honored to meet and work with Jill at a time in her life when she was wanting to make a real difference. When we first met, she shared that she was worried her daughters were wanting to buy more and more games, toys, and clothes. She shared that though she hadn't spoiled her daughters, there was pressure to buy, buy, buy. It was important for her to set an example of giving back for her girls.

Jill

Jill is a divorced mom with two daughters. She works about fifty hours per week as a secretary at a busy contracting company. She and her ex-husband get along fairly well. He is a good dad and takes his daughters to his apartment every other weekend.

Jill doesn't have a lot of time or money to give, but she told me she felt it is important to do her part as a positive role model for her daughters. She told me about her daughters coming home from school and sharing about their community service projects. One project was to help repaint the school library and to start a book drive for the town library. Jill remembered having done similar activities when she was growing up, but admitted to having become less involved in the community since raising two daughters, mostly on her own.

When she began writing in her Generosity Journal and answering questions about her vision, Jill noticed a recurring theme: children's health. While she cared about all aspects of children's well-being, she was most focused on this issue. When Jill's first daughter was born, the baby developed a respiratory infection that almost took her life. Those days were long for Jill and her husband at the time. She credited her family's health insurance and good doctors and nurses for saving her daughter's life. Not surprisingly, that time had always stayed with Jill. She began to think about those parents inside and outside of the United States whose children didn't have access to the same level of health care.

I asked her what was wrong with the system, what she felt was broken, and where she thought hope lived.

As she wrote, Jill said she thought about her daughters, and her eyes filled with tears. She then imagined her daughters having children and wondered if they would have the resources they needed to care for them. With her job, Jill wasn't be able to save a lot for her daughters. She said she then imagined her great-great-grandchildren. What would they want her to hope for? What would they want her to work for? What could she do that would make them proud of her? Though she may not be able to pass on a financial gift to them, what giving roots could she pass on?

Thinking of these children she might never meet and of the children who were already going without, Jill wrote:

Children are our most precious resource. The life of a child changes adults into parents and parents into grandparents. Children are our legacy and our hope for a community that we have started to build and that they can make better. I envision a world where all children have healthy food, clean water, affordable health care, and I envision a world where we have the will to make this possible. That will starts with me.

After writing her vision, Jill set her priorities and chose the organizations she believed to be most committed to this vision. Today, Jill talks about the new level of significance she feels in her life and the sense of pride she gets when she and her daughters sit down to read a newsletter from a children's health organization. They talk about how much money they'd like to give to this effort and then post the thank-you letter on their refrigerator.

Of her vision statement, Jill said, "If someday my great-great-grandchildren read this, I hope they'll be proud of me and feel that I did my very best for them and for all of God's children."

One of the gifts of Jill's vision statement is its impact on her daughters. They were so excited about their mom's new undertaking that they wanted to write their own vision statements to figure out what they could do to make a difference. While both girls said they were happy to help with the library book drive, that wasn't what they cared about most. For one daughter, it was helping animals in shelters; for the other daughter, it was the environment.

If you are a parent or grandparent reading this book and want to help your children or grandchildren create a Generosity Plan with the family and/or help them have their own mini-Generosity Plans, try this tip that was helpful to Jill and her daughters:

Each family member should create her or his own vision statement. Then share your responses with each other. By doing this, you will see the threads that connect your giving as a family and the uniqueness that you bring as well. As you progress through this book, you will find ways to give as a family and to give separately. In Jill's case, she gives to children's health, and her daughters give a portion of their allowance to a local animal shelter and to an environmental protection group. As a family, they listen and learn about one another's cause, and once every six months, they volunteer at one family member's favorite charitable cause.

Vision Statement 1
(written by baby boomers Molly and Jim)
We envision a world where hope, fairness, and opportunity are the norm, and hopelessness and despair are in the past.

Vision Statement 2
(written by college student Jess)
I believe in a world where discrimination is a notion of the past—one that is read about in history books—and people value each other for their uniqueness and wide range of talents.

Vision Statement 3
(written by retirees Margaret and William)
We can see a world where education is at the top of federal, state, and local budgets, and every child has a safe, supportive environment in which to learn and grow.

As you create your vision statement, use the vivid, idealized descriptions in the chart on the next page to motivate and inspire you. Think about why these vision statements matter so much to the choices these individuals make in their day-to-day lives. For the retired, married couple who wrote the third vision statement, they are clear that children and education are their top priorities. They aren't saying that other areas are unimportant; they are saying they believe this is a smart and needed area to support, and the possibility of this vision coming true inspires them.

In addition, by naming their vision, they have already begun to set their priorities. All three of these visions were set by people who know what they stand for and what they want to support. If they are then approached by a friend who is raising money to, say, start a community garden, they may provide a little support, but they know they should give within their primary passion in order to be most effective. We'll talk much more about this in chapter 4, but for now, keep in mind how your vision statement plays into this.

My personal passion is animal rights and women's rights, but neither of these may be your passion. What's most important is that I am living and giving to my passion, and I want you do to the same. When we give to our heart-and-soul work, we stay the course, we dig a little deeper, and—to reflect Mahatma Gandhi's words— "we become the change we wish to see in the world." Plus, there are so many important causes. It does my heart good knowing that there are individuals just like you who prioritize the arts, music, education, democracy, children, disease prevention, disease cures, voting rights, and so much more. We will all sleep better at night knowing that each of us is focusing on our passion, our area of expertise. When we dilute our efforts, we are not effective. We are most effective when we focus.

Your vision statement should reflect your passion and should serve your needs, so take the time to make sure it does. You will then have a more effortless and fun time with your Generosity Plan, just like Stephen, Jacki, and Jill and her daughters. Now, before we move to setting your priorities, the final tip for creating your vision is to take ten:

> *Take all the internal resistances that arise when you begin to envision* (that will never happen *or* my kids will think this is ridiculous). *Put aside negative thoughts. In about ten minutes, you can come back to them if you need to. Until then, just take a ten-minute vacation from their limiting impact on you so you can think from a visionary place. Remember: in your vision, anything is possible and all is achievable.*

Now, with your personal, family, or group vision fully unlocked—or becoming unlocked—you are ready to set your generosity priorities. With the setting of these priorities, your Generosity Plan will begin to take real shape. You will start to see how the work you have done thus far is reflected, and you will begin to add content to your plan.

Setting Your Generosity Priorities

Prioritizing your charitable focus areas is a helpful tool that will allow your giving roots to thrive and your vision for the world to blossom. When we set priorities, we more efficiently apply our time and resources. When we don't set priorities, we find we take on more than we can handle and feel we're not making headway.

This happens a lot when New Year's rolls around. We feel we have a clean slate and will get to all those things we didn't get to in the year prior. However, we tend to pile on quite a few resolutions: lose weight, get in shape, spend less money, spend less time at work, spend more time with the family, read more, watch less television, learn a foreign language, find a better job, find a different apartment, adopt a dog. All of these are noble endeavors. Alas, when we try all of them at once, come February, we find ourselves in front of the television, eating potato chips after a ten-hour workday that did not include going to the gym.

We're not failures; we've just taken on more than we can handle. However, if we set priorities, choose two or three undertakings, and then spread them out over the year, we are going to feel more accomplished and more effective, and we can trust that we'll follow through on the goals we set.

This applies to generosity as well. In the United States alone, there are an estimated 1.5 million nonprofit charitable organizations. This averages to thirty thousand per state. Imagine the number of causes these thirty thousand groups represent. We cannot be effective if we are trying to learn about, volunteer for, or write checks to all of them. Trust me. I've tried, and I've been ineffective. I've spread myself too thin and made promises I couldn't keep because I felt every cause mattered. However, I am one person who can do her part. And that is all that is required of each of us: to do our part.

Setting priorities will ensure that you are not spreading yourself too thin and that you are still participating to the best of your ability. More importantly, defining the reasons and motivation behind your giving further enriches the sense of personal rewards. For those of us who feel like there is so much to be done and not enough time or funding, investing in your own priorities and seeing results in them will calm your personal worries as you put your plan into action. Donna, a woman I had the privilege of working with, found that her desire to honor her brother's memory helped shape her focus in the area that mattered most to her.

Donna

In the 1990s, Donna's brother was struck with Lou Gehrig's disease, or ALS. He fought hard but succumbed to the illness at an early age. Donna was devastated. During his illness, she spent time learning everything she could about the disease. She wanted to know what he was experiencing, the results of the latest research, the hope for a cure, the long-term prognosis for patients, and the long-term prognosis for the disease.

After her brother passed away, Donna took a break from reading literature. Having lost her only sibling, she felt lost. But as she began to heal, she felt strong enough to reconnect to the ALS community and get caught up again.

When we met, I helped Donna to write her vision statement using the same steps you are following in this book. Her vision statement focused on the illness, of course, but I was struck that she talked about "reducing" and "alleviating suffering" twice in her statement.

With her vision statement in hand, we ventured to set her priorities. To help her, I asked her to do the same that I have asked of you: Look closely at your vision statement. Through what means do you want to help move that vision to reality? To Donna I asked: Is your passion funding research for a cure? Lobbying governments and the private sector for more funding? Raising visibility and awareness through education and publicity? Supporting better end-of-life care for those afflicted? Supporting friends and family affected by this disease?

When I asked the last two questions, Donna looked up from her Generosity Journal. Her face froze, and then she began to cry. Reducing and alleviating suffering for all affected by ALS were Donna's priorities. While she believed wholeheartedly in increased funding, research for a cure, lobbying, education, and advocacy, Donna's passion was to provide care and emotional support for those living with—and through—this devastating illness.

For Donna, setting priorities meant getting clear about where specifically—within the whole field of ALS—she wanted to make a difference. She knew that she would give her all to helping patients and their friends and family. She remembered her brother's suffering. She remembered her own. Her vision was a world without this illness and absent of suffering by those afflicted and affected. Her priorities matched her vision. Her priorities helped her get specific. Her priorities helped her know where she wanted to volunteer and what she wanted to fund.

In each of our passion areas, we can make a difference in countless ways. If your vision is to ensure that children have healthy, nutritious food in abundance, you could support groups that feed children; you could volunteer to lobby for increased federal, national, and private funding; you could host local events to raise awareness; you could connect with middle schools and high schools to galvanize young people's involvement; you could write letters to multinational corporations asking them to give 1 percent more in the fight against childhood hunger. The engagement possibilities are endless. The key is prioritizing your involvement. You have created your vision and you know your passions; now, determine your greatest interests.

For Donna, her interest was family support, physical therapy, and hospice for the person with ALS. If it were you, you might choose to focus on research, alternative medicine, education, or support for veterans or those serving in the military who have ALS. Again, each matters. Each is important. You are welcome to divide your financial contributions to one, two, or even three of these areas. What's important in this process is knowing which of the areas within your cause moves you the most—motivates you into action. The charts on the following pages show how Stephen, Jill, and Anne set their priorities to support their vision statements and maximize their impact.

Setting your priorities may require a little research, but you won't need to put in hours and hours. You know your vision, your interests, and your values. You can simply type your passion areas into a search engine and start to get a sense of what is out there.

For me, there are countless ways I can be involved in animal rights: ending cosmetic testing; supporting spaying and neutering;

Stephen's Vision Statement	Stephen's Priorities
I believe in a world where every single person should have the same opportunities and the same access to learning, earning, music, and the arts. I believe that governments can work each day to serve the needs of their people and that real fairness begins when real democracy is practiced.	1. Education: making sure his alma mater's school curriculum teaches classes on the dangers of tyranny and supporting those institutions that prioritize music and the arts 2. Advocacy: organizations that promote democracy locally, nationally, and internationally 3. Entrepreneurialism: especially those organizations that support young people to help maximize their lifetime earning potential

helping end the sale of endangered, exotic animals. Once I got clear about which areas of animal rights and animal protection I cared about, I did a little more research, just like Donna did. I could start writing letters to companies still testing mascara on rabbits or raise funds for animal sanctuaries for abused or neglected wildlife. If need be, spend some time researching, ask friends you know who are already involved, and/or sign up for a few online e-blasts or newsletters to read more (you can always unsubscribe later!).

Use your Generosity Journal to list out your priorities. If you need time to discover them, make a list of three to five things

Jill's Vision Statement	Jill's Priorities
Children are our most precious resource. The life of a child changes adults into parents and parents into grandparents. Children are our legacy and our hope for a community that we have started to build and that they can make better. I envision a world where all children have healthy food, clean water, and affordable health care, and I envision a world where we have the will to make this possible. That will starts with me.	1. Children's health care: local medical clinics providing direct care and national groups I can trust that work on legislation and provide hands-on opportunities for my daughters and me 2. Clean water: local clean water initiatives and products that reduce waste and promote new initiatives 3. Healthy food: healthy products for my local pantry and support for the WIC (Women, Infants, Children) program

you need to do to determine what you'd like to learn (Are there local groups doing this work? Can people at a community organization or church or synagogue share with me what they are doing? Which organizations welcome children volunteers?).

You should be very proud of having come this far. I have met billionaires who haven't taken these steps when it comes to practicing philanthropy. By going back to your roots, unlocking and naming your vision, and setting your generosity priorities, you have already made leaps and bounds toward making a difference in the areas that you care about most. Because of these efforts, the shift in you and in

Anne's Vision Statement	Anne's Priorities
That women and girls have the right to their rights always; that global crises, like genocide, are prevented; and that a cure for cancer is realized	1. Women's rights: on-the-ground groups that help women secure property rights and employment, as well as health and reproductive rights organizations 2. Genocide prevention: grassroots organizations that work to promote community rights and international organizations that help to eliminate poverty 3. Cancer: research, education, and clinical trials

the world is already taking place. Now, because of this good work, you are ready to learn that you have always had the keys to changing the world inside of you. With a strong foundation and commitment to doing your part, you can now take the next step toward applying your unique gifts and talents to changing the way the world works, for the better.

Remember to take the time you need to create your vision statement and name your priorities. As you move forward, you will be glad you made the time to get clear and focused. Your confidence will increase, you will be more enthusiastic, and getting involved will cease to feel overwhelming.

3
How to Change the World
Time, Treasure, Talent, and Taking a Stand

Time: *noun*, a continuous, measurable quantity in which events occur in a sequence proceeding from the past through the present to the future

Treasure: *noun*, stored wealth, or valuable or precious possessions of any kind

Talent: *noun*, natural abilities or qualities

I first heard the phrase "time, treasure, and talent" in my early twenties. Wanting to learn everything I could about fundraising, I had signed up for a free fundraising teleconference call on "Increasing Donor Diversity in Your Database." The man leading the call was a development professional who fundraised primarily in the African-American community. The goal of the call: how nonprofits can effectively diversify their funding base to include a wide range of communities of color.

While he spoke, I took many notes. I wrote down his favorite strategies and recommendations. I was moved and excited when he stated, "At my organization, we engage all of our donors by inviting not just their wallet to the table but their time and talents. Our success is based on the African-American view of philanthropy—time, treasure, and talent."

After the call, I became more deeply involved in philanthropy in the African-American community, other communities of color, and in the Global South. In many of these communities, large monetary gifts did not alone define philanthropy. Like the philanthropy that I learned through working with and for grassroots organizations, this philanthropy welcomed and needed all types of offerings to make a difference.

For example, in fighting for civil and basic human rights, the African-American community recognized all gifts as critical, as Yvonne M. Brake notes in *Black Philanthropy*:

> *In addition to their roles as church-goers, African-American citizens made enormous formal (through nonprofit organizations and associations) and informal contributions during the civil rights movement. Their philanthropic gifts were the heart of the movement, ranging from participating in boycotts to helping organize NAACP events to providing meals for Freedom Riders registering Southern voters to taking in children of lynching victims to marching on Washington to becoming the first to desegregate schools.[3]*

The time, treasure, and talent model works because it takes all of our gifts in service to the greater good. Together, they can transform money into action, time into outcomes, and talents into possibilities. Alone, they are less effective.

Imagine treasure alone: Picture a community with $1 million in the bank but no board of directors to make sure that money is properly stewarded and well spent. Imagine $1 million in a community with no volunteers to turn that money into food for hungry families. Money alone doesn't make a difference. For money to work, it needs our time and our talents.

Imagine time alone: Picture an auditorium filled with individuals ready to give blood to support the local hospitals. Without the funding to advertise the blood drive, pay the nurses, keep the blood stored safely, and transport the blood to emergency rooms, the auditorium would be filled with well-meaning volunteers who couldn't help. Without the talents of nurses and health care practitioners, we would not know how much blood to take per person or what the volunteer needed after giving blood. For time to work, it needs our treasure and our talents.

Imagine talents alone: Picture laboratories filled with researchers working on a cure for diabetes. They have the training, the smarts, the know-how, and the readiness to find a cure. Without the funding, they have no equipment, no computer modules, no vaccine compounds, no clinical trials. Without volunteer time, they wouldn't have a board of directors to oversee their work or fundraise for the research. Without volunteers to raise money through bike-a-thons and walk-a-thons, the researchers would not have a broad base of support to make their dream a reality. For talents to work, they need our treasure and our time.

In our personal lives, the time, treasure, and talent model also works. We apply all three of our gifts when we purchase and upkeep a home, raise children, take care of animals, and take care of ourselves. When we find we are lacking one of our precious resources—like time or money—it can be difficult and stressful to make progress in our lives. It can even cause us to lose momentum on our goals or stall us right when we are making headway. Our personal affairs are at their best when resources steadily and consistently funnel into our lives.

As this is true in our personal lives, so it is true in charitable work and in making social change. This model of giving was further brought home to me by a woman named Clara.

Clara

Clara is a woman of strong faith. She believes that the gifts she had to offer—her time, her treasure, and her talents—are not gifts that belonged to her. Clara believes that her job as she passes through this lifetime is to make the most of the gifts given and entrusted to her by her God. When she gives, she doesn't expect plaques or her name in lights. Giving is her way of caring for her fellow brothers and sisters, as well as honoring the gifts she feels fortunate enough to have received.

Clara feels like a rich woman—in all the ways she feels a person can have richness. Clara has a good family, work she enjoys, caring friends. She has never gone without a place to live, food to eat, books to read. She loves to play board games, and she loves to give back.

Clara raised four children, worked part time, helped care for her grandchildren, and managed her house. Despite her full schedule, she felt she had ample time to give back. She was not rich by U.S. standards, but she believed she had enough treasure for herself and her family, with some to spare. Clara is also a gifted pianist and has taught this skill to her children, grandchildren, and—because she believes in giving her talents—to children in her community who couldn't afford lessons.

When I first read the quote by President Theodore Roosevelt, "Do what you can, with what you have, where you are," I wondered if I was really doing my part, if I was living up to my fullest generosity capacity. When I heard about Clara, I knew for sure she was.

Because Clara sees her time, her financial resources, and her talents as gifts she is stewarding, giving them is effortless. She also believes that while the giving of one offering could help a little, giving all three could help a lot. As Clara said, "What good are our gifts if we don't fully share them?"

Some of the best and most powerful examples I know of the time, treasure, and talent model at work include athletic-based fundraising events and faith-based giving.

From Special Olympics to bike-a-thons, walk-a-thons, and charity road races, participants give their time, treasure, and talent to make a difference. If you are new to the sport, you must train for it. When you want to give up or fear you don't have the talent, you imagine the people or animals behind the cause, and you give *that* much more. You fundraise per mile walked, run, or biked. You give your time to learn how to fundraise and to ask friends to support you. You give your time in training and on the day of the event. As a result, we witness what can result when each of us gives to our capacity: we see our favorite cause getting much-needed funding, visibility, and support.

What could make activities like these even more powerful is participants finding a way to continue to give their many gifts to the cause long after the event is complete. If you are a walker, biker, or runner, what ways could you use your talent to raise awareness or funds throughout the year?

Let's say you ran in your first 5K and are now training for a 10K. Could you try to double the funds raised since you are doubling your mileage? Or could you aim to walk six miles in your own informal walk-a-thon and ask friends to sponsor you (even if it's just you out there!) so you can then give the money raised to your favorite charity?

Think about the creative ways you can use your athletic talent to benefit your favorite cause—not just once a year but throughout the year. Like in our personal lives when a steady and consistent contribution of our own time, treasure, and talent makes our lives work better, the same applies for our Generosity Plan and to making the world a better place.

And as for faith-based giving, members of organized religious bodies may be quite familiar with the time, treasure, and talent model. If you belong to a church, this model may be the basis for the church's annual fundraising campaign or it could be the model used to orient new members about making offerings to the church.

From individuals I have talked with who are active in church, some have shared a concern that the time, treasure, and talent model doesn't always yield results. Some churchgoers have told me that during an annual campaign, they are asked how they can volunteer their time to benefit the church and how they can apply their talents to help members of the church community. And if you know your talents and have applied them in the past, it may be relatively easy for you to figure out your talent plan. However, if you haven't had as much practice or don't see yourself as a natural leader, you may be wondering what you could possibly have to offer. You know the value of giving all three of the Ts, but you can't see exactly how to make it work for you.

The opportunity here is to know that each of us has talents that are important and meaningful and that we should think of people's talents in an expansive way: Who in the church is a good listener? Who has a knack for making people feel at ease? Who would be a good buddy to a new member who is shy?

Oftentimes the people who have had more practice or who are self-starters quickly find a way to get involved. For those individuals who don't quickly identify a concrete talent, we need to look a little deeper at their qualities, characteristics, and offerings.

If you are involved in a church, ask yourself: What talents in my congregation are not quickly visible but are valuable? What heart-based talents does the church need to help fulfill its mission? Who can I talk to in the church to ensure that steps are taken to involve everyone?

We feel the full benefits of the time, treasure, and talent model when everyone gives to capacity. To reach our full generosity potential, we only need to broaden our definition of talent. When we do, we will likely witness something extraordinary.

If you're not sure exactly how you can uncover your time, treasure, and talent capacity, all you have to do is begin somewhere. Sometimes, by giving one of our gifts, we can carve out the giving of all our gifts. This happened for Maryann.

Maryann

In Seattle, I worked with a volunteer who contributed her time, treasure, and talent to a produce reclamation program we had launched. The goal of the program was to rescue edible but not sellable fresh produce from wholesalers and, within a few hours, get it into the hands of men, women, and children visiting local area food pantries. For many reasons, the program became a huge success, and to this day, it rescues and delivers more than one million pounds of fresh produce to greater Seattle's hungry families. Many individuals, donors, businesses, and organizations made this program the success it is today, and Maryann was one of them.

When Maryann learned about the program, she wanted to be involved right way. At first, she said she didn't have any money to give. She had been on food stamps and had benefited from the food bank. And though she now had a full-time job, she was trying to get back on her feet. Still, she felt she wanted to give back to the food bank and was excited to learn about this new program that got fresh, healthy food into the hands of people in need.

Maryann was also concerned that she didn't have the right skills or talents for the program. She told me a number of times that there was probably someone better qualified to help out, but she shared that she was willing to learn and do any job that needed to be done.

Maryann began by giving her time, which was invaluable.

As the program progressed, we invited SkyCity Restaurant at the Space Needle to get involved. We shared that for many of the families at the food pantry, cooking with fresh produce was a luxury they hadn't been able to afford before. Now, they had bags of colorful and nutrient-rich produce, but were uncertain how to cook with it to benefit their families. We asked if the SkyCity chefs would be willing to come to a food pantry and conduct demonstrations using the fresh produce. They loved the idea and immediately said yes.

Maryann volunteered the day the chefs arrived. She helped as they plugged in their frying pans and, in their tall white chef hats, whipped up easy and delicious meals using only the ingredients in the food pantry. Maryann handed out samples, talked about how she had learned to cook with fresh produce, and shared how her own health had improved now that she was eating more fruits and vegetables.

Maryann's talents for educating and inspiring came shining through. Just a few months into the program, Maryann was giving her time, her talents, and her treasure to help make the program a success.

While it may feel challenging at first to imagine your gifts to help make a difference, the key lies in two places: play to your strengths and expand your definition of *talents*.

At first, Maryann didn't see that she had talents as an educator and a trainer. However, without even knowing it, she played to her strengths: her gratitude to food banks, her passion for getting healthy food to hungry people, and her willingness to do the right thing.

This gratitude, passion, and willingness got Maryann to give her time. As she grew, so did the program, and vice versa. The rewards she felt by giving her time, treasure, and talent were far greater than if she had given one gift alone.

†††

When you think about contributing your time, treasure, and talent, what opportunities do you see available to you? Where do you get stuck (*I'm a graphic designer, but no nonprofit I've called needs free graphic design services*)? What creative ways can you think of to help you get unstuck (*instead of calling nonprofits at random, I'll ask my friends and colleagues if they know of any organization needing free design work and if I can arrange a meeting*)?

When thinking about contributing your gifts, call on your friends and others to help you figure out ways you can get involved and use your best skills to benefit your favorite cause.

The time, treasure, and talent model works. It will work for you. Simply take some time to jot down ideas in your Generosity Journal and talk through them with people who support your decision to make contributions. Remember to play to your strengths and gifts. What you have to offer is needed.

Taking a Stand

When we think of taking a stand for a cause we believe in, many of us think of grand and noble people and grand and noble gestures: the great activist Rosa Parks, who took a stand about equal rights for people of color by taking a seat on a public bus; Mother Teresa, who took a stand for the poor of Calcutta by relinquishing all personal belongings and leading a life of service. These acts are extraordinary. They captured the sign of the times, catapulted much-needed societal change, and inspired the rest of us to feel hopeful about the future. However, much like big money philanthropy, it can be difficult to feel that taking a stand is available to all of us, especially if we think of taking a stand in only big ways for big causes.

What, then, does it mean to take a stand if you're not the leader of a social movement or a known figure within a global cause? What does it look like to take a stand if you're working full time? If you're raising children? If you're busy getting out of debt? If you're building a career, or if you are a shy or quiet person?

To take a stand, you simply need to know and believe in these two concepts: stand and voice.

The literal and metaphorical definition of *stand* is "to occupy a place or location." For the cause you care about most, taking a stand means to occupy a place within that cause. You don't need to occupy the top place. You don't need to be the sole voice yelling from the top of a building (unless you'd enjoy that—just make sure you get a permit). What is required of you is to stand somewhere within the cause.

Know why you care about the cause so much, why it means so much to you. Know what about it breaks your heart. Know what about it helps you be hopeful. By taking a stand, you add fuel to your cause. You step up for that which you care about most.

Taking a stand won't be a big leap for you. If you've given your time, treasure, and talent to your favorite cause, you have stood for it: through yourself, your checkbook, and your skills. Now, where do you stand within your cause? Where is the place for you, and where do you want to stand? Think of others you know who take a stand. Instead of mimicking their style, think of why their stand works. If you know someone who keeps a blog about her favorite cause—like a cure for breast cancer, help for those suffering with mental illness, or reducing carbon emissions—what about her makes taking that type of stand work? Is she a writer? An extrovert? Is she opinionated? Is that why this type of taking a stand works?

What about you? How will you loudly or quietly stand in your cause? What actions would have you feeling that you truly stepped up for your greatest passion?

It's clear that knowing where you stand and giving your time, treasure, and talent translate into *taking* a stand. Now, to add greater influence to your cause and to deepen your own commitment, you should look at adding your own unique and powerful voice to your cause.

The dictionary definition of *voice* is "the ability to speak." When it comes to having voice for a cause, I define *voice* as "the ability to speak through words, sign language, art, music, performance, written word—any way that you give voice to something greater than you."

While at times bringing voice to a cause can show up as expressing anger, discontent, frustration, or being against an action or a policy, voice can also be positive and powerful. Take my dear friend Amanda. When she speaks of providing mentoring to new, young moms, her voice around this issue is that these are smart, capable women who can excel and soar and whose children can have an extraordinary life, no matter the starting circumstances. For Amanda, voice is not about regretting how a situation came to be or whose fault or what system created the problem. For her, voice is a powerful and positive future.

When it comes to your greatest passion, how do you define voice? How do you express your voice for your favorite cause? How can the expression of your voice help you stand within your cause?

For me, expressing my voice at the Four Seasons Hotel in New York City more than a decade ago helped me to stand within my work in a whole new fabulous way. What I learned is that, for me, the expression of my voice means holding my dignity while not robbing others of theirs. Here's what happened:

I was fundraising for a cause near and dear to my heart. A donor friend gave me the contact information for her friend, who we'll call

Maria. I contacted Maria, told her who referred me, and asked if she'd like to get together to talk about the organization. She gave a resounding yes.

On the day of our breakfast, I arrived early to the Four Seasons—a place I had never been before. Glancing through the menu, I saw that bagels were $14. (Note to self: order water.) Moments later, a woman walked in the front door. She was looking around. I was thinking, *That can't be her*. This was for a very progressive organization. The woman approaching me had a lot of hair, even more makeup, and was wearing a full-length mink coat and stilettos first thing in the morning. She walked right up to me. "You must be Kathy," she said. "I'm so sorry I'm late!"

The busboy ran over to us, saying her table was ready. Fourteen-dollar bagels, a fur coat, and her own table. I was one intimidated fundraiser. As we made our way, me just behind and left of her, she pulled off her mink coat and, without turning around or looking at me, reached back her arm and handed me the coat.

If you've read the book thus far and aren't just joining us, you've already learned that I am an animal rights person. A *big* animal rights person. As that full-length mink coat came toward me, I felt I was in the moment that lasted forever. One part of my brain was saying, *Just take it. Take it. Take the coat. You can complain about rich people back at the office later*. The other part of the brain said, *Oh boy, I have to tell the truth, don't I?*

Later, when I thought back on this moment, I understood what was happening for me: was I fundraising for social change, or was this an opportunity for social change while I was fundraising? I chose the latter.

I leaned forward and put my hand on the small of her back. "Can I tell you something?" I asked.

She stopped, turned slightly, and said, "Sure."

"I would love to take your coat, but I am a huge animal rights activist and, the truth is, doing so would freak me out. However, how about if I find someone who can take both our coats?"

Her head was bowed down. Then she looked up at me. I saw her eyes were filled with tears, and I thought, *I'm fired*. She then said, "Do you know why I was late today? First, it takes a long time to look this way, and I've got my husband's reputation to uphold. Second, our friend told me you were pretty smart about this stuff, and I was a bit intimidated."

She was intimidated? Leading up to our breakfast and up until I shared that I couldn't take her coat, I was terrified—terrified that I wasn't sophisticated enough for this meeting. Scared that I would get it wrong, she wouldn't write a check, and we wouldn't be able to fund an important program because I blew it. Who would have guessed that we were both struggling with our voices and our places in this world?

What followed after I said, "I'm just glad I didn't hand you *my* coat to hang up, because the inside is held together with duct tape," was one of the nicest breakfasts of my fundraising career. We shot straight from the hip and the heart. She wrote a check, I made a friend, and together we made a difference. I found my voice that day and knew from then on that I would not have to check myself, or my coat, at the door.

That day at the Four Seasons, I took a leap of faith and expressed my voice. Thanks to Maria's generosity and graciousness, we both learned that we are all much more similar than we are different, especially when we are working toward the greater good.

How do you express your voice? Through words? Art? Music? Writing? For many of us, expression happens most powerfully not alone but together.

Consider the individuals behind the AIDS Memorial quilt. They took a stand and creatively expressed their voice about those lives lost to AIDS through one panel of patchwork at a time. When each artistic piece was sewn together, what started as one panel became forty-seven thousand.

After Hurricane Katrina, volunteers and musicians came together and gave their time, treasure, talents, stand, and voices to build housing for families and musicians. I was fortunate enough to see firsthand the musicians village on Alvar Street in New Orleans. It was not a surprise that the folks who bring us music that fills our souls, together with the good people of Habitat for Humanity, created bright, colorful, vibrant houses painted in purples, blues, greens, and yellows.

In both these scenarios, results came in all shapes and sizes, but each stemmed from time, treasure, talent, and taking a stand. While both of these efforts are a testimony to generosity, we needn't wait for tragic circumstances to create possibility.

In Greenfield, Massachusetts, nine other women and I launched the Women Investing in Women Scholarship Program. Each of us was able to pay for college because of the generosity of others who funded scholarship programs. We benefited from those scholarships, and none of us has forgotten this investment in us and our futures. Coming together, we saw that while we wanted to give much-needed funds to women students looking to secure their associate's degree, we also wanted to apply our time and our talents. By using this model, we created a program in which women could intern at our consulting firms or companies. They would learn business skills while pursuing their academics. This skill sharing was particularly important to us as a group because no matter our career paths—advisers, artists, business owners, managers—we all benefited from learning how to turn our passions into our life work. We wanted scholarship recipients to secure a wide range of skills to achieve their academic goals and to make their lives as successful as possible.

Some of us also volunteered to meet with scholarship recipients to be an ear and a guide. Of course, in the process, we have learned as much from them—maybe even more than they learned from us. These are smart, caring, committed women aiming to reach their fullest potential. The gift of this program is allowing the time, treasure, and talent model to lead us. In doing so, we stand in the cause we care so much about—affordable education for women—and express our voices not alone but as a chorus.

For you, what does standing in and for your cause and voice have to do with generosity? What are the benefits of taking a stand and expressing your voice as a group versus as one person? What are opportunities you see that could allow you to express voice and take a stand with others?

Remember, there are no wrong answers. The most important part of these exercises is the process of you creating just the right role and just the right venues to share your many gifts.

4
Choosing Charities
Naming the Causes You Care About Most

I know that for many, the word *charity* brings up a host of associations, some positive, some less positive. We're going to spend a little time looking at the word *charity* and determining what it means to you. Taking this time now to understand charity and exactly the types of efforts you want to support will help ensure that your time, treasure, talent, and stand will have the maximum impact.

For some, *charity* carries a positive association. As a noun, it indicates "an organization working to help those in need." As an adjective, as in *to be charitable*, it means "to be generous to those who are going without or are suffering." Taken further, *charitable* also denotes "graciousness," meaning to be kind or lenient in our judgment of others. I'm certain that we've all been grateful when someone has been charitable with us, even if they don't agree with our point of view or we have been less than charitable in our opinion of them. In general, most view charity and the act of being charitable as favorable. Few could argue that we should not help those in need or that we should not act kindly toward others.

At the same time, some are less comfortable with the word *charity*. In the 1920s in the United States, those who asserted that aid to the poor should go beyond basic services were called progressive reformers. These reformers "argued against the poverty-relief approach to social services and put forward a social justice approach ... [including] minimum-wage laws and workers' insurance."[4] Today there are charitable groups throughout the world that work every day to ensure that those living in poverty, or those facing intolerable conditions, are given food, clothing, and shelter and are also given a fair chance to build the lives they deserve.

Today, when we discuss poverty relief, the discussion goes beyond solely providing direct aid. Many agree with efforts to provide collateral-free loans to poor people to help them create income-generating projects or start their own businesses. Even more agree in investing in literacy and education and providing children with health care. These efforts encourage social service and social change.

For some who work in and for social justice and transformation, charity can be viewed as harmful in that it can keep afloat a system in which the rich help the poor but conditions don't change. They argue that the status quo keeps those suffering in a permanent position of suffering.

While this book won't cover the debate and discussion around charity versus change versus justice, this brief overview is included because it is important to determine what the word *charity* means to you so that your Generosity Plan can be as meaningful as possible. As you get more involved in the cause you care about, you will learn what you need to know to help advance its important work. This learning will help open the possibilities of your generosity and help define how and in what ways you will be charitable. To find the right match for you and where you will soar, I urge you to be as charitable as you are capable of being. Be charitable to those benefiting from your generosity. See everyone as a person who has unique talents to contribute. Allow the deepest notion of charity to become a practice or habit in your life. Then, whichever philanthropic road you choose, you will be on the right one for you.

Ayesha

When I asked Ayesha how she defined charity and how this definition informed how she gave her time, treasure, talent, stand, and
voice to the world, she spoke beautifully and eloquently, almost
magically. Her lens helped to expand my own notion of giving
back and making a difference.

As Ayesha reflected on our conversation about charity, she
went back to her own giving roots. She examined more deeply her
family's traditions of giving, looking closely at how she came to
determine what charity and generosity meant to her.

She wrote me this letter, which I'll share with you. (You'll see
why I didn't change a word.)

One of the five pillars of Islam is zakat, *translated as charity or social
justice. Pillars hold up a roof and allow one to build a strong structure
upon the foundation. Charity is therefore a core spiritual value that is
critical in building a life of strength, compassion, and generosity. While
zakat starts at 2.5 percent of one's annual savings, one is encouraged to
give 10 percent or more if able.*

*But not being able to give that amount is no bar to participation!
Everyone can be a part of giving because it goes far beyond money to
encompass the way we carry ourselves in the world: by feeding people,
saying a kind word or granting the benefit of the doubt, and even smil-
ing at someone. The spiritual seeker hopes to achieve the level of* ihsan
*[beauty/excellence] where the honey of these principles becomes so
much a part of one that it flows through one's veins, sweetening one's
every thought, word, and action.*

*One of the first acts done on behalf of a Muslim child when they
are born is that the hair on their head is shaved and the equivalent
weight in gold or silver (depending on what the family can afford) of
the hair is given to those in need. So we literally give of ourselves (hair*

in this case) to spiritually signify that charity is most meaningful when we give of our essence and our gifts. It isn't only about monthly or annual gifts then; it is also about the cultivation of daily generosity of words, heart, thoughts, soul, wealth, and action.

But in order for us to be charitable with others, we first need to be so to ourselves. We need to love ourselves and feel fulfilled in order to love and give to others. We need to take time out from our busy lives to reflect upon what our needs are and how to fulfill them, because otherwise we will endlessly consume and fill our homes with material goods to hide the inner emptiness or pain temporarily.

In a world that never stops, charity—beginning with generosity toward and listening to one's self—gives us the chance to pause and ask ourselves: What is enough? How do I make the most of this moment right now? How can I use my gifts and time positively and powerfully?

Once we have drawn the "enough" line, we can stop living in fear of scarcity. We can begin offering up our time, listening, money, and smiles from a place of generosity, sharing, and service. Someone once said that "service is the rent we pay for life." I think service is what makes our souls grow and [that it] is inextricably linked to charity.

Embracing charity and service as a part of our daily lives deeply roots us in our communities, and connects us inwards to our passions and outwards to the human family. So many of us feel aimless or powerless. We often look at those with more wealth than ourselves and feel poor, or feel that if only we had their connections we could do some "real" good in the world.

For real inspiration, look at those with less material wealth than yourself. My parents took us to Pakistan annually from the San Francisco Bay Area, so I was able to experience village life firsthand as a child. Seeing people with little material wealth but incredible generosity and spiritual wisdom deeply impacted me. They are still the standard I hold myself to.

Pakistanis are incredibly hospitable, and it's quite common for them to invite complete strangers into their homes for a cup of tea. It's hard to imagine that here in the U.S. when so many of us don't know our neighbors or live in fear of strangers. But I was often invited into small mud houses in which small children played next to chickens and an open fire. My hosts usually had very little to go around, but all that they had they were willing to share generously—even if it meant less for them later. By accepting a cup of tea in a tin mug accompanied by a couple of syrupy, neon-colored sweets, I was acknowledging them not as someone poor or less-than, but as my generous host. That created a space where we could meet as equals eager to connect, me with much to learn and she with much to offer.

Such generosity is both humbling and inspiring. There are so many tales to tell of my years living there: A Pakistani widow with little financial security but the few gold bangles she wore, took them off to offer them for the nation's debt-relief campaign. Sheer generosity *and* bravery. Mukhtar Mai saved one out of every two rupees she earned so that she could open the only school for children in her area. How many of us have ever witnessed charity of that magnitude?

While the Gates and Buffets of the world certainly awe one with the sheer magnitude of their giving, that widow and Mukhtar Mai, and millions of others like them around the word, are feeding, educating, and caring for communities that government or development dollars may never reach.

In the mid-'80s, my parents gave up lucrative careers in the U.S. to move to Pakistan and serve its people. My two sisters and I, all under thirteen years of age, also moved at that time. My parents believed that the "loss" in lifestyle standard would be more than made up for by the adventures we would have there—and they were right. My father served as a cardiologist for twenty years at a hospital that provided free care to those in need, and my mother ran an organization that taught widows and girls economic skills so that they could contribute to their families and societies in healthy and dignified ways.

My parents' examples—and the Islamic principles which inspired them—have been my guiding lights in thinking about and engaging with charity as both social justice and generosity of mind, body, and soul.

Kathy, I shared with you that it was only when I was on disability due to a (now resolved) health issue that I began giving away 10 percent of my income. I continue that practice now, and it amazes me that now that amount feels like only the beginning. I hope to do more in the future and am currently thinking about ways to make that possible. There are so many ways to give and to be engaged. The more one gives, the more one feels fulfilled and rooted on this Earth. As Omar Mozzafar said, "When we think we have love, yet we take, that is not love. When we truly have love, we give and give and give. And that giving cures us of so many discontents in our hearts and lives."

My great-grandmother used to tell stories from Nature to illustrate spiritual principles. One of her parables was that the more heavily laden a tree is with fruit, the more deeply it bows to God in gratitude.

It's a compelling image that has stayed with me. The tree that is deeply rooted, grows tall, spreads an inviting and protective shade, and bows low with heavy, sweet fruit which it offers to and shares with all those who pass by, generously and continuously.

That image embodies charity for me.

Be open to what it means to you to live a charitable life. Like in chapter 1, where you went back to your giving roots and uncovered from whom you learned about giving back, this chapter offers you the opportunity to be expansive in your notion of charity. Equally important, it asks of you to be charitable, which means to not sit in judgment of how others choose to share their resources. Instead, you have the chance to put your heart, soul, and resources toward your greatest passion. If that is toppling a regime, go to it. If it is feeding hungry people, get started. If that is advocating for better conditions for elderly people, I thank you. If that is giving your resources to your alma mater, the institution is stronger for it. Charity—in all its shapes, sizes, and permutations—asks us to be a better person than we were yesterday.

Being charitable also invites us to be gracious. To live a charitable life means to offer respect to someone else's charitable work or cause, even if you don't share the same views. As you live your most generous life, you will feel more fulfilled and more satisfied not in changing other people's minds or values to match yours, but in respecting theirs as you ask yours to be respected.

For you, what is the value of charity? What does it ask of you? Do you feel you have an obligation to help those in need?

What does it mean to be a charitable person? Can you recall a time when you were charitable toward something even though you didn't understand it? Can you recall a time when you were less than charitable? What opportunities await you today to be charitable?

Years ago, I had a good laugh at myself. While on the way to volunteer my time, I slammed on my horn and yelled at the person in front of me to go. I'm pretty sure I yelled something like, "Hurry, I'm trying to get somewhere to help someone." That day I reminded myself that on the road to helping, I might want to be charitable.

Choosing Charities

Once we know what being charitable means to us, we can be more effective in choosing organizations or efforts that best match our hopes, personality, and interests.

Remember that even if an organization has two or three qualities you are looking for—say, a local organization that helps women who have survived breast cancer—it may not necessarily mean you will find it a match for you. To be sure it's the right fit, you need to know what else you're looking for in an organization or initiative.

Finding the right effort to stand in is a bit like finding a date. If you were to sign up on an internet-based dating site, you would fill out a form about you. You'd include your gender, age, profession, likes, dislikes, where you live, and more. The internet dating folks would then begin to suggest matches for you. They may find someone who shares similarities with you: age fifty, been married once, enjoys outdoor sports and travel. While you'd be hopeful that there could be a good dating match, you're not likely to show up on the first date with a wedding ring and the color scheme for your new house. Instead, you're likely to take this hopeful starting point and see if there are deeper connections, like values, hopes for the future, and life plans. Then, as you've gotten to know your initial match, you can decide if there isn't compatibility beyond zip code and love of running, or if there is a real foundation for dating and more.

If you apply a similar approach to choosing efforts where you want to give your time, treasure, and talent, you will surely be more fulfilled and more connected to your heartfelt charitable work. I have had many eye-opening experiences with philanthropists of many backgrounds who experience a subtle shift in their philanthropic compass. As they begin to put their plan into action, many have found that their true passions emerge as their experiences become more personally challenging. What does this deepening look like?

"Paula"

Let's imagine that you are Paula, a retired teacher, with a passion for learning. While you no longer have the stamina to teach full-time, you do want to lend your time and talents to one or two children in need. In particular, you want to help young people who—when given extra time, attention, and instruction—could produce great results.

You know of the local organization in town that provides out-of-classroom tutoring to students. You don't know much about them except that they have a good reputation for helping students get good results. Armed with enthusiasm, you head to the tutoring offices and sign up to tutor a young person. You complete volunteer training and orientation, and in no time at all are assigned to a seventh-grade boy struggling in science. You are excited and raring to go.

However, as the program progresses, you discover a lot of what you call mismatches. For this organization, the driving measure of success is graduating students from the classes as quickly as possible and sharing success stories with donors and the public. Where initially you had been impressed with their numbers and results, now, inside of the organization, you are feeling that quantity (number of students graduating) might be trumping quality (depth of learning). Your approach to teaching is thorough, methodical, and time intensive. You are thrilled if a student can quickly and easily grasp a learning concept. However, your value system tells you to take the time needed to get the job done right.

The organization you are volunteering for operates a different model of student learning than yours. While you are a savvy person and can appreciate the organizations' more fast-track approach to instruction, when it comes to learning, you identify as old school. For you, the fulfillment comes in seeing a student have new skills, confidence, and readiness to advance to his next level of learning.

Now, after volunteering for five months (and quieting the voices in your heart that said, *this may not be a match*), you realize that this organization is not the right place for you. What do you do? You want to volunteer. You want to give back. You feel disheartened. The town you live in is small, and you don't feel you have the time or the stamina to drive to neighboring towns. But you want to mentor. What is the opportunity here to hone your philanthropic compass?

If you are Paula, you can widen your search to find matching values. To find the most fulfilling volunteer experience, realize it may not always present itself out of the gate or from the place you'd expect to find it. Dig a little deeper. Put the word out to friends and family that you are making yourself available as a tutor. Share the kind of tutor you are and the approach and skills you bring to teaching. Call your former school to learn if a student or two could benefit from extra tutoring during study halls or after school. Call the local Boys and Girls Club to find out about available teaching opportunities. You can even call a for-profit company whose aims and values match yours.

During this search, be specific. Lily Tomlin said, "I always wanted to be someone. Now I realize I should have been more specific." Interview as much as you are being interviewed. Share your hopes, what you bring, where you need support, which students you would and wouldn't be a good match for. For example, could you work well with a student who is distracted and can't sit still for long? Is that student the right match for you because you were just like that in school? Or do you match better with students who are quieter or shy? Taking the time to ask the right questions will help ensure a value match that you will need in order to be fulfilled by and satisfied in your experience.

As you think about your charities of choice, what do you already know that you are looking for? Go back to the early pages of your Generosity Journal to review your thoughts and ideas from chapters 1 and 2. What other qualities are you seeking when you think about giving your time, treasure, and talent? Do you need to know how an organization is spending the money that is donated? Are you interested in learning how the organization measures success?

To help you, use the chart below and on the next page to help you create a profile of your perfect match. Put a check mark next to those that mean the most to you:

I am most interested in giving my time, treasure, and talent:	The types of organizations I believe are critical to support (Remember, "types" as in not *what* they do but *how* they do it):
☐ Locally ☐ Regionally ☐ Nationally ☐ Internationally ☐ All of the above	☐ Social service organizations ☐ Social change organizations ☐ Educational/art institutions ☐ Advocacy groups ☐ Research and/or science ☐ Faith-based ☐ Media/technology/social networking ☐ All of the above ☐ Other: _____

The organizational qualities that matter to me include:	The elements that I believe must be present for success include:
☐ Number of individuals benefited from the services ☐ Overall benefit to the community ☐ Overall benefit to the country ☐ Overall benefit to the world ☐ Percentage of money spent on overhead/ administration ☐ How results are measured ☐ Immediate results ☐ Long-term results ☐ Other:_____	☐ Inspiring leader who is an expert in the mission ☐ Programs or initiatives that I can read about but don't need to be a part of ☐ Programs or initiatives that I can be a part of or involved in ☐ A competent and effective board of directors that is open and honest ☐ Constituents who are benefiting ☐ How long the organization has been around ☐ Financial stability of the organization ☐ Taking risks ☐ Not taking risks

To help you create your own statement for choosing your favorite charities, review the examples on page 69. Then, based on your answers to the checklists, take a moment to answer, "The issue I care about most is . . ." then, "I am most interested in. . . ."

Here's what's great about these exercises: You may find that there are a lot of organizations out there that you are drawn to. Fantastic. It is rewarding to see possibilities, explore them, and begin to

---

EXAMPLE 1

The issue I care about most is: feeding hungry children.

To support this cause, I am most interested in giving locally to groups that provide direct service. While I don't necessarily have to provide hands-on support, I do want to know how the group defines success, and I want to know that the people in charge understand what the problems are and the best way to solve them.

EXAMPLE 2

The issue I care about most is: providing educational opportunities to the poorest people in the world.

I am most interested in faith-based groups that work around the world. I would want to know that the group has been around a while and that it is focused on immediate results and long-term impact. I would want to be involved in some way and am open to learning about what ways the organization involves volunteers.

EXAMPLE 3

The issue I care about most is: a cure for cancer and Alzheimer's disease.

I am most interested in research organizations. I care less about how much is spent on overhead and am more interested in using the money where it is needed to get results. I would want to know that the groups employ experts and that they share their findings with other organizations.

---

refine your matches. Take the time you need. Remember, there are no wrong answers. There is only what is right for you.

Alternately, you may find you have a very clear idea of what you are generally looking for. Also great. If you are clear and sure about this, you are primed and ready to move on to chapter 5. If, however, you are still exploring the right charitable match for you, you can still create the statement that best reflects your interests, passions, and values for now.

Like "Paula," Tricia wanted to volunteer locally. She created her Choosing Charities statement: *The issue I care about most is animals, especially domestic animals and wolves. I am most interested in local organizations that provide direct service, and national organizations that advocate for animals and educate the public.* Tricia felt almost ready to proceed. She just had one last match to check: values.

Tricia

When Tricia decided to volunteer locally, she knew she wanted to look no further than the area animal shelter. While her financial contributions supported national efforts to raise awareness, she knew that locally she could be involved hands-on. While looking for a shelter to support, she found two. Before she looked at how many miles each was from her work, its hours of operation, and what volunteer opportunities were available, she looked at the type of shelter and whether it euthanized animals that were not adopted—if it was a no-kill shelter.

Tricia is grateful to those volunteers who can work in shelters that perform euthanasia. However, for her, after working for more than a dozen years as a veterinary technician, she felt she had seen her share of animals put to sleep. While she understood that this approach can be a necessity and didn't judge those shelters that might have been forced to take this measure, she knew that her heart would break in this type of facility. She told me she couldn't imagine seeing the same dog every Monday night for weeks on end only to come in the following Monday to an empty cage, not because he was adopted but because no one ever did adopt him.

In choosing the place to volunteer, a no-kill shelter was the right values match for Tricia. She knew that in order to be an effective volunteer, to stay with the organization for the long haul, and to have a true impact, she would have to choose one that matched her values.

What key values are you looking for in your giving experience? For Jacki, who is interested in women's issues, it was finding women's organizations that celebrated women of faith. For Michelle, who is interested in food banks, it was finding a food bank that didn't just feed hungry people but had programs in place that helped to end hunger.

Like Paula, Tricia, Jacki, and Michelle, you have the chance to deepen your Choosing Charities statement by enriching it with your values. Use your Generosity Journal to name the values that are a match for you, then add these values to your Choosing Criteria statement. Read it out loud to someone. Does it ring true? Is anything missing? Do you feel excited and jazzed by it?

My personal Choosing Criteria is:

I look for endeavors that are bold, entrepreneurial, and trailblazing. I like to get involved in projects that can best open new ways of looking at odd problems. I look for bright, compassionate leaders who know their stuff and move forward strategically and fearlessly.

Your Choosing Criteria statement is a reflection of your vision, hopes, values, and generosity. Make it your own, and you will certainly find the right organizations and efforts where you will no doubt thrive.

Generosity Plan Built for Two

What do you do if you and your partner or spouse are at different ends of the Choosing Charities spectrum? For best results, play to each other's strengths, like James and Andrea did.

James and Andrea

James and Andrea had different ideas about what criteria must exist in a nonprofit for them to give their time or treasure. They also brought very different values to the table.

Andrea was interested in adding "heart, soul, and spirit" to a nonprofit or charitable effort. James, on the other hand, wanted to make sure his support went to real results that could be seen and measured.

They argued some about which approach is better, and both made the case for their point of view. Eventually, after much debate, they saw the value not in one approach over the other, but in combining both perspectives. They decided to see each other's values as strengths rather than as a "cold" approach or an "ineffective" way of getting things done.

As a result they decided to write a check to a charitable initiative that met both their needs: a rooftop garden at a children's hospital. For Andrea, it ensured that sick children would access "nature, warmth, and spirit" instead of merely seeing sterile rooms and even more sterile equipment. For James, it worked because it was something tangible for the kids, it was for an institution that had a proven track record of results. With only one point of view, their Generosity Plan would not have been as creative or effective. However, by combining their strengths, they found just the right match for their individual and shared values.

If you are giving treasure with a spouse, children, or a small circle of friends, how can you combine the values and best thinking to create a truly transformative charitable experience?

Getting to Know the Nonprofit World

Now that you have your Choosing Charities statement, you want to make sure you have a general feel for the nonprofit sector. This section includes the most frequently asked questions about nonprofits. You can find more information about these types of organizations on my website, kathylemay.com.

If you feel you know what you need to understand about nonprofit organizations, you have permission to breeze through this section. If, however, you feel it could benefit you to read up on the hows, whats, and whys of the nonprofit sector, I strongly encourage you to continue reading while making notes in your Generosity Journal. Pay special attention to the types of nonprofit organizations that are out there and how to gauge if they are truly making a difference.

Remember, if you want to know what will happen with your financial contribution, ask. If you want to make sure your time spent will be effective, ask how and in what ways your time contribution will be valuable. If you want to be sure your talents will positively benefit your favorite cause, ask about the best way to apply them. For your most effective Generosity Plan, there's no substitution for raising your hand and doing your part to make it work.

Now let's learn some of the basics.

Kathy LeMay

What is a Nonprofit Organization?

A nonprofit organization is any corporation, trust, association, cooperative, or other organization that:

1. is operated primarily for scientific, educational, service, charitable, or similar purposes in the public interest;

2. is not organized primarily for profit;

3. uses its net proceeds to maintain, improve, or expand its operations.[5]

Does this mean that nonprofits can't make a profit?

No. In fact, most nonprofits that end each calendar or fiscal year with a deficit (expenses exceed revenue raised) can experience greater difficulties in meeting program goals and their overall mission. Ending a calendar or fiscal year with net revenue increases an organization's capacity to make a difference. "What distinguishes nonprofits is not whether they can make a profit but what happens to profits. Nonprofits are prohibited from distributing profits in the same way for-profit corporations can. All revenue must be earmarked for the organization's mission," which includes reasonable expenses like programs, office space, and staff salaries.[6] In short, a legal nonprofit corporation cannot distribute its profits to individuals who have control over the overall operation, like members of the board of directors or the advisory board.

How many nonprofits are there in the United States?

According to the National Center for Charitable Statistics, as of 2008, there were 1.5 million nonprofits in the United States.[7] If nonprofits were evenly distributed among the fifty states, this would translate to thirty thousand nonprofits per state.

Of the total nonprofits, 974,337 are 501(c)(3) public charities (defined above) whose missions and programs relate but are not limited to: arts, culture, and humanities; education; environmental quality, protection, and beautification; animal rights and welfare; diseases, disorders, medical disciplines; civil rights, social action, advocacy; science and technology research institutes; religion-related spiritual development; community improvement; philanthropy, volunteerism, grant-making foundations; and international, foreign affairs, and national security organizations.

Another 115,340 are 501 private foundations, each of which is defined as "[receiving] most of its income from investments and endowments. This income is used to make grants to other organizations rather than being disbursed directly for charitable activities."[8]

And 446,457 are other 501(c) nonprofit organizations, including civic leagues, social welfare organizations; business leagues, chambers of commerce; labor, agricultural or horticultural organizations; social and recreational clubs; and veterans organizations.

Don't nonprofits get most of their funding from governments or foundations?

Nonprofits rely primarily on individuals to fund their work. In fact, of the $283 billion contributed to nonprofit organizations in 2007, 81 percent came from individuals.[9]

As of the writing of this book, with the election of President Obama and the resulting stimulus package, more government funding may again become available to social service and social change organizations. However, the best model for nonprofits is a healthy balance of government, foundation, individual, and corporate support.

Aren't nonprofits small, charity-based groups? How much impact can they really have?

The nonprofit sector is a vital component of the U.S. economy. Nonprofits employ eleven million people, or 7 percent of the U.S. workforce.[10]

In fact "83.9 million adults volunteer 15.5 billion hours each year towards community and public benefit, the equivalent of 7.7 million full time staff." For comparison purposes "the total active military personnel in all services (Army, Navy, Marines, Air Force) total 1.4 million."[11]

How are nonprofits held accountable for their spending?

In recent years, nonprofit organizations have received more media attention than in years prior. At one time, the work of nonprofit organizations could be found in the "special interest" section of the newspaper or during an end-of-the year giving drive. Attention was usually favorable, as it spotlighted groups helping members of a community. These days, the media attention can be less than favorable.

The public has expressed concerns over issues like inflated over-head costs, overpaid executive directors, and too many nonprofits in one arena, resulting in duplication of services and financial irregularities. I address these briefly on page 82, but for now, take a look at this list of the bodies responsible, according to Independent Sectors, for the governance and accountability of nonprofit organizations:

- **Boards:** All nonprofits are governed by a board of directors or trustees (there's no real difference), which is a group of volunteers that is legally responsible for making sure the organization remains true to its mission, safeguards its assets, and operates in the public interest.

- **Private watchdog groups:** Several private groups (who are themselves nonprofits) monitor the behavior and performance of other nonprofits on a local, national, and international level.
- **State charity regulators:** The attorney general's office or some other part of the state government maintains a list of registered nonprofits and investigates complaints of fraud and abuse.
- **Internal Revenue Service:** A division of the IRS (the Tax Exempt/Government Entities division) is charged with ensuring that nonprofits are complying with the requirements for eligibility for tax-exempt status. [If an organization is audited and found to be in violation, it could have its tax-exempt status revoked or be charged fines and taxes.]
- **Donors and members:** Some of the most powerful safeguards of nonprofit integrity are individual donors and members. By withholding their financial support, donors can strongly encourage nonprofits to reappraise their operations.
- **Media:** Many nonprofit leaders may feel misunderstood or even maligned by negative media coverage. However, this media watchdog role has resulted in increased awareness and accountability throughout the sector.[12]

  Note from the author: The media plays an important role in making great nonprofits visible and exposing nonprofits that are unethical. At the same time, the media aims to get headlines. Sometimes complexities within the nonprofit world can't be captured in a print story, so read between the lines when you read a story about a nonprofit in the media.

To this list, I add *you*! By asking good questions and requiring transparency, you can help ensure that nonprofits live up their promises and maintain their integrity.

It should be noted that these bodies don't always guarantee against improprieties. As in the for-profit sector, some individuals do not operate within the true spirit of the company's vision and mission. However, nonprofit corruption and fraud is minimal, especially compared to the size of the sector.

Now for the big question.

Is My Money Making a Difference?

With good reason, this question is one of the most asked about the nonprofit sector. The following information will help you understand how nonprofits measure impact and how you can determine if, and in what ways, your donations are making a difference.

To help us we'll revisit our earlier discussion of social service versus social change organizations. Once you can differentiate, you will feel more confident writing checks and giving time, and you will know what results you can expect and why.

Social service organizations

Direct service organizations may seem to have the easiest time assessing impact. For example, a food pantry can state how many people it was able to feed as a result of food and cash donations. A crisis hotline can share how many calls were received and evaluate the role of volunteers and staff in meeting the needs of the callers.

At the same time, social service organizations face unique challenges. Let's say you run a food pantry. It provides food, groceries, and vouchers to individuals and families who are food insecure. Because your primary mission may be feeding hungry people rather than ending hunger, the expectation is that delivery can happen by volunteers and your overhead can remain low. For this food pantry, how do you define success and impact? Let's say, in the year 2000, the pantry served five hundred individuals and families. Then five years later in 2005, the food pantry reported that it doubled the number of families served, from five hundred to one thousand.

To some donors this may read as successful. They think, *Because of the pantry's outreach and efficiency, it is meeting the needs of more hungry people*. Other donors may read this differently: *Did the number of hungry people double in the five-year period, or did the food pantry grow to meet the need? Is the food pantry really reaching everyone who needs it?* Still others may have a different perspective: *Is it success to serve more people? It's not good news that five hundred more families are hungry or that those families went without for so many years*.

I share this example to illustrate that measuring impact—even in what might seem the most straightforward circumstances—is not simple. What one person may consider success, others may consider an unsettling trend.

Social change organizations

The definition of a *social change organization* (and *social change philanthropy*, which funds this work) is a group that "creates change in the nature, the social institutions, the social behavior or the social relations of a society, community of people, or other social structures."[13]

For example, while a food pantry functions as a social service organization that feeds hungry people, a social change organization works to eliminate the conditions that create hunger and food deprivation. In short, social change is systemic change that works to remove the root causes of the problem. A social change organization works to create the conditions for all to succeed versus a social service organization, which helps those who are in need. Social change organizations work toward the day when the playing field is level and no groups of individuals are left out or left behind (i.e., children, women, communities of color, animals, indigenous people).

Examples of social change organizations include:

- **Children's Defense Fund:** The Children's Defense Fund's Leave No Child Behind® mission is "to ensure every child a Healthy Start, a Head Start, a Fair Start, a Safe Start, and a Moral Start in life and [a] successful passage to adulthood with the help of caring families and communities."[14]
- **Women's Funding Network:** As a worldwide partnership of women's funds, donors, and allies committed to social justice, the Women's Funding Network seeks to ensure that women's funds are recognized as the "investment of choice" for people who value the full participation of women and girls in society.[15]
- **CANDI Cats and Dogs International:** A social entrepreneurial model that aims to eliminate stray animals, change attitudes around cats and dogs through programs supported by the tourism industry, travelers, and pet lovers.[16]

How do organizations like these measure impact? If you are giving your time, treasure, or talent to one of them, what results can and should you expect as a result of your contributions?

Benchmarking progress and success

When you invest in social change, you won't see hard evidence of the return you get from investing in a social service, which might tell you, "Your contribution of $45 will fund twelve immunization shots for children in need." The key to successful funding of social change lies in understanding the organization's long-term goals and how funding incremental benchmarks will help to meet those long-term goals. I know, not very exciting stuff, but making change for the better is a task that requires a different approach than does social service.

As an example, let's look at the smoking cessation movement in the United States. Those who led this effort knew that they had to change attitudes and culture before they would see a reduction in the number of new smokers. While many of us would want to see our charitable gifts immediately result in fewer smokers, the social change element inherent in this initiative would first require investing in education and outreach to change the thinking about smoking. Rather than setting short-term goals, organizers created a long-term plan with benchmarks, including changing perception that smoking is good for relaxation and decreasing advertising to children and teenagers. These benchmarks helped to establish progress, determine challenges, and seize opportunities.

Key to the success of their work: education. How do you determine who has been educated and the impact of that education? Will people who fund the work feel a difference has been made if the organization states, "With your funding, we published, printed, and distributed one million brochures"? The questions that would follow: To whom were the brochures distributed? Were they targeted to adults or to young people? Were they in multiple languages? How do you know they were read?

To change the culture around smoking, the smoking cessation leadership created multiple strategies on multiple levels. They knew that brochures left sitting on the shelf of a library or in a youth center would not transform attitudes. Instead, they built partnerships with educational and faith-based organizations. Working with community leaders, they created campaigns to motivate young people and women to quit smoking. They developed programs aimed at ensuring young people and women who didn't smoke didn't pick up that first cigarette. Teachers, doctors, counselors, faith advisers, parents, and coaches talked with kids about the dangers and cost of smoking. The movement raised community awareness, helped shift attitudes about smoking, shared with kids what they could afford if they weren't buying cigarettes, and helped women take control of their health and well-being.

Still in process, this movement has been in motion and action for decades. What does this mean? Social change takes time.

It took time for the movement leadership to determine which groups to target and why, how to combat messages that show smokers as healthy and sophisticated, what it takes to change culture, what can be learned from other movements, whether regulation could be the answer, and how to be conscious of personal will and rights. The folks who led and stood in the smoking cessation movement knew it would take time to shift attitudes and see real changes. Today, most restaurants are smoke free. More adults and young people are trying smoking cessation tools like gum and the patch. Doctors no longer tell stressed-out patients to smoke; they advise exercise.

If you want to know what is happening in your cause, be it curing cancer, helping war veterans, preserving the culture of First Nations, ask. Ask the groups you care about to tell you where there is progress and why, where there are hurdles and why. Read more. Become an expert. Take the time to learn what you need to know. Who knows? You might just have in you the answers we've all been seeking.

Overhead Costs and Accountability

An effective nonprofit has a low overhead. The more it spends on programs, the bigger difference the organization will make.

This is not always the case. If we were to gauge an organization by percentage overhead only, we would miss out on the big picture. It costs money to run an organization. Low overhead doesn't necessarily translate into high impact. In fact, it could be argued that if a nonprofit has very low overhead (say, 5 percent) that organization could be under-investing in its employees or getting services donated that could soon expire. The most important metric in a nonprofit organization is mission fulfillment. If it costs a little more to achieve the mission with the best talent to deliver programs, that may be well worth the cost. Should nonprofits spend 40–50 percent on overhead services? Of course not. However, remember that the generally accepted 20–22 percent works if an organization is a direct service or charity and most of its staff are volunteers.[17] If it's a social change, advocacy, or think tank, human resources are its most valuable and, sometimes, most costly resource for meeting the mission.

Nonprofits lack good entrepreneurial skills and a sense of productivity and accountability. Like government employees, they're drawing salaries unrelated to performance.

"By definition, nonprofits must be entrepreneurial, productive, and accountable. Their funding operations require recruiting members, acquiring donations, receiving grants, and operating profitable commercial enterprises. Indeed, they must be entrepreneurial in order to raise sufficient funds to survive and grow. Like most companies, they work within annual budgets. Similar to thriving businesses, nonprofits must increasingly advertise their activities and vigorously market their products and services. However, nonprofit entrepreneurialism differs from private sector entrepreneurialism in that it disproportionately centers on raising funds and recruiting members. Nonprofits also must be productive and accountable in relation to board members, who set policies, approve budgets, and oversee operations. Nonprofit productivity is measured differently from business productivity. Similar to government productivity, nonprofit productivity is measured in reference to organizational goals. Nonprofits are increasingly under pressure to clearly state their missions in terms of measurable goals as well as to be more and more accountable to their boards."[18]

As you choose charities to benefit from your generosity, you may find that while nonprofit organizations are one place you will contribute your gifts, they may not be the only place. You may choose to be more involved in your faith-based institution where you already know the inner workings of how decisions are made. You may also choose to help out within a for-profit entity that is looking to include charity as part of its outreach.

However, if your Generosity Plan includes building a relationship with a nonprofit organization, the more you know, the better your experience will be. Refer to this section as needed to keep you thinking about the right questions to ask and some of the ins and outs of nonprofit organizations. You will also find additional resources in the appendix.

Whichever way you get involved—be it with a small, local organization or with a larger, international organization—know what you expect and what you are seeking to accomplish. While it's a bit of extra work up front, you will have already used the time portion of your Generosity Plan wisely.

Course Correction

If you find that a nonprofit or charity that once seemed like a fit no longer resonates with your core beliefs and Generosity Plan, you have the right to change course. Moving on to a new experience doesn't negate your important efforts. I used to think that in order for something to have value, it needed to last a lifetime. In the field of social change, I've learned instead that my commitment is to living a generous life and to helping create conditions for the better. As with relationships that come into your life, as the saying goes, for a reason, a season, or a lifetime, so do relationships evolve with charities.

As I have developed in my own philanthropy, I have learned when it is time to let go and move on. In one instance I got involved with an organization providing opportunities for young women. After learning about the work, getting to know others involved, and seeing the organization's programs firsthand, I made a contribution that was significant to me. As part of my time, treasure, and talent plan, I put my fundraising skills to work, visiting with other donors and inviting them to match me at my giving level. I was excited to use my fundraising skills to leverage my gift and increase its capacity to help more young women.

While I had hoped this could be a lifetime commitment, as year one moved into year two, I wasn't fulfilled in my relationship with the organization. Though I asked for them, I didn't receive many program updates. On two of the donor visits, the staff member who accompanied me offended the donors we were meeting with. The organization regularly asked for more of my time than I had told them I could give when we started working together. They also called me often to say they weren't going to meet budget and ask if I could introduce them to "people with money." I began to feel like a rolodex to the organization rather than a valued friend and supporter. I shared with them my concerns and what resulted was no contact from that point forward.

While communication had broken down, it was still difficult for me to leave for several reasons: the organization was a match for my priority area called "women and girls," its mission resonated with me, and it was effective in the programming. However, organization leaders clearly had a different idea of working with volunteers and donors than my fundraising practice. Plus, their leader often seemed more frustrated with "lack of progress" than inspired by progress being made. Because of these reasons, the organization was no longer a match for me. It had come onto my philanthropic path for a season, but it was not destined to be in my Generosity Plan for a lifetime.

From this experience, I learned that I needed more than just a strong mission statement and good programs in order to feel fulfilled and connected. By moving on, I was able to focus my energies on organizations that better matched my approach to working with donors and volunteers. I am inspired by these organizations and am therefore able to be as generous as I can be.

Know what matters to you and what conditions need to exist for you to be happy and fulfilled. Remember, one size does not fit all. You can find what you are seeking; you simply need to put in a little time to making sure you find your match. Trust your instincts. In the long run, you'll make an enormous difference.

5
Finding the Time to Give Your Time

Making a Difference through
Just the Right Volunteer Experience

*W*hen it comes to volunteering, I tip my hat to women. Sorry, guys, but long before volunteering was seen as a powerful and effective commodity, women gave time in droves. In fact, in the year 2008 alone, according to the United States Bureau of Labor Statistics, "Women volunteered at a higher rate than did men across all age groups, educational levels, and other major demographic characteristics.... Overall, 36 million women perform[ed] unpaid volunteer work."

Walk into any hospital gift shop or cafeteria in the United States, and behind the sundry items and food counters, you will find women ringing up teddy bears and making grilled cheese sandwiches and tomato soup. On election day, women take their places in gray folding chairs behind eight-foot wobbly cafeteria tables, signing in seasoned and new voters and guiding us to tiny little booths that promise democracy. In libraries, women restock shelves, explain the Dewey decimal system, and point us to the right book stack for that one special book we are seeking. Women pass out food at food pantries, remind us to give blood at our local blood drive, help out their neighbors, walk down the street to teach literacy, and travel around the globe to dig ditches, launch micro-credit programs, and provide support where needed. When it comes to volunteering, women hold up more than half the sky.

Of course, men volunteer too. My dear friend York, after a successful business career, decided he was ready to move from "success to significance." For the next five years, he served as president of two nonprofit organizations. York worked full time and never took a dime.

Given that men do volunteer, why the emphasis on women giving time, and what does this emphasis mean for your Generosity Plan? I place this emphasis on women's giving of time to broaden your own definition of contributing. There are two ways to give time: formal and informal.

With the vast and growing nonprofit sector, many of us give our time through formal or structured programs. Formal types of giving time include mentoring a young person, volunteering at a soup kitchen, sorting clothes at a Salvation Army or Goodwill, or reading to patients at a hospital or to the elderly in a nursing home.

At the same time, giving your time happens informally every day, all over the world. And, according to statistics, it is women who more often than men give of their time in this way. With formal volunteering, hours contributed get counted, and you are most likely helping out strangers. With informal volunteering, hours contributed don't get counted, and you are most likely helping out friends, family, neighbors, or coworkers.

Both ways of giving your time matter. If you do one but not the other, you will surely make a difference. However, giving both will help you feel fulfilled and connected in a whole new way and will help you in the practice of generosity.

When you give your time informally, you help family, friends, and neighbors, but you may never help a stranger. At the same time, when you give formally—serving on a board of directors or stocking cans at a food pantry—you know the joy of helping out strangers, but you miss out on the gift of unplanned, "uncounted" giving. When you do both, you experience new sides of yourself and recognize the power of giving time whenever possible, in all possible ways.

Amanda

My friend Amanda is married with two children. Her first and foremost priority is her role as mom and spouse. Her secondary love is her work as a personal trainer. Amanda grew up in New York City where she lived a financially privileged life. However, when it came to giving, her parents didn't attend big galas or $1,000-per-plate dinners. For them, the most important part of giving back was giving of their time and themselves. They did this both formally and informally.

Along with her parents and brother and sister, Amanda would spend holidays at nursing homes. They'd arrive in the morning with wrapped gifts, smiles, and energy and would spend the day with the residents, talking, singing, eating dinner, laughing, and opening presents. Through this formal giving, Amanda learned the power of making a difference through direct work with strangers.

At the same time, Amanda's mom showed her what it meant to give from the heart simply because it was the right thing to do and because she could. Sending her off to school, Amanda's mother would often pack more food than she could eat during one lunch period. Her mother would say that if that day she needed all the food for her strength, then she should eat it, but if she found she didn't need it all, maybe she could consider sharing it with someone who was going without. Amanda did just that. Over the years, walking to school, she stopped and shared apples, sandwiches, and juice boxes with people who were homeless and who she had gotten to know on her way to and from school. She did this for years. Toward the end of high school, she expanded this practice of giving by bringing blankets with her boyfriend to the friends they had made, and by treating these friends to coffee and sharing conversation at nearby shops.

Through this practice of giving, Amanda lived the adage, "Do what you can, with what you have, where you are." She had extra food to share and, just as importantly, she shared her time. None of this time was counted by a census bureau, but this time definitely counted for the people she met. It counted for her.

"My father used to say, if we can help feed people who we've seen over the years and gotten to know, then we should. I'd like to see their faces twenty years from now." Of these early experiences, Amanda said she learned about the humanity in herself and in others and about the power of one person to live up to her giving potential.

When giving of your time, you have an opportunity to know the people you are sharing your time with, whether they're people without housing, people who are food insecure, individuals living with life-threatening illnesses, or children with learning disabilities. Your world will be enriched as you get to know the people behind the causes.

My favorite illustration of this lesson comes from a piece titled "Lessons for an Activist from a White, Republican Male":

Dan Leonard is an activist with all the right credentials: he's been to Palestine, he's worked with the poor in Uganda, he could claim roots in a notoriously poor neighborhood of Philadelphia. Leonard's father is a "middle class, Republican, suburban evangelical." In an essay in the latest issue of Geez, *Leonard dissects his years of "empire-toppling activities," an exercise inspired by a transformative moment on a bridge with his father:*

"On my most recent trip home, fresh back from Palestine, I met my father outside the train station. The bridge leading from the train station to my father's office is home to many homeless folk, and as we approached [the] bridge, I reached in my pocket for change with the intention [of] proving something to my dad. But as we crossed the bridge, I noticed that each homeless person we passed greeted my father by name.

"He was a celebrity on the bridge. And not a single person asked him for money. It occurred to me that he did something few activists do—walk the same path five days a week for 30 years.

"We stopped and talked to one woman, Rona. My dad introduced me, and she mentioned that she had heard all about my upcoming marriage and my work with the church. She was not particularly interested in my work with the poor but instead told me how wonderful my father was.

"I realized later that for all the times I had protested in support of the poor, not one poor person in Philadelphia knew me by name."[19]

The lesson here is to be in relationship with those who are benefiting from your time. This young man had been formally volunteering but didn't include informal one-on-one connection in giving his time. He worked to support the poor, but he didn't know a single person he was advocating for. What his father taught him is a lesson that can guide each of us: strangers only stay that way if you don't introduce yourself.

What kind of volunteer experience are you ready to have? The following questions will help you explore ways you have given your time informally and formally, and ways you'd like to give your time as you move forward. The stories and advice that follow will focus primarily on formal volunteering, as finding the right formal opportunity is often more challenging than helping a friend or family member in need.

1. **How have you given your time informally?** List friends or family members you have helped.

- *I helped a younger sibling with homework.*
- *I volunteered at a coworker's fundraiser for a school.*
- *I walked a neighbor's dog without getting paid.*

Think about how you have helped lift a burden or stress for someone you know. What did you enjoy about this experience? Was there something about the experience you didn't enjoy? Would you give your time to something like this again?

2. **How have you given your time formally?** List organizations or initiatives you have helped.

- *I serve on a board of directors for my favorite cause.*
- *I volunteer weekly for a rape crisis hotline.*
- *I host an exchange student every summer.*

What did you enjoy about this formal giving? Was there something about the experience you didn't enjoy? Do you want to continue giving time in this way? If you haven't yet volunteered formally, write ideas you've had about giving your time. What do you hope the formal volunteer experience will bring?

3. **What would be your ideal volunteer experience?** Don't worry if you think you're not qualified. Simply write what your dream volunteer job would be.

- *I want to work overseas helping endangered species.*
- *I want to volunteer at the Olympics.*
- *I want to train to become a teacher and teach in an isolated rural community.*

Use your journal to remember how you have given your time formally and informally. Note what has and hasn't worked for you and what you hope for in the future. If you'd like to try out a volunteer experience but feel a little nervous, ask a friend or coworker if he'd like to volunteer with you. Giving our time has unlimited application. What's the right volunteer opportunity for you?

Finding the Right Volunteer Opportunity for You

Amanda

For Amanda, who grew up in a family that practiced formal and informal volunteering, the challenge in finding just the right volunteer opportunity presented itself when she started a family of her own.

As a single person with a history of family volunteering, Amanda easily made volunteering part of her life when she became an adult. Before getting married and having children, she had an easy time finding ways to volunteer. She knew her passions—young moms, the chronically ill, and dyslexia—and found formal and informal ways to help.

When her son and daughter became old enough to be involved, she wanted her whole family to volunteer together to continue the giving legacy instilled in her by her parents.

So she started calling service agencies. She called homeless shelters, food pantries, and soup kitchens. She called local hospitals, libraries, and universities. She spent hours on the phone trying to find a way for her family to volunteer. Unfortunately, the agencies didn't have a way for eight-year-olds to volunteer; the minimum age was thirteen or fifteen.

Amanda felt stuck and discouraged. Here she was, combing the phone book for a way for her family to get involved. She knew they could host a canned food drive or raise money for a charity, but she wanted the opportunity for her family to make a difference on a personal level. She wanted her kids to lead with their hearts.

Then her friend told her about the Fresh Air Fund. The Fresh Air Fund matches young people who live in New York City with host families who live in or near the great outdoors. Families host a young person for a week, providing them with fun, fresh air, and a great outdoor experience.

For Amanda, this was just the right match for her and her family. Here's why:

- Positively impacting one person's life built on her family's giving traditions.
- Exercise and the outdoors is the whole family's passion.
- The child they hosted lived in New York City, where they lived prior to moving to their new home.
- Her youngest son would be an integral part of the experience.
- Her whole family would experience the power of giving time together—in this case 24/7—in support of one person's life.

To make it work, the family discussed it: What are the pros? Cons? Concerns? Hopes? Was everyone willing to commit to the project and this young person for a week? What could they do as a family to make this a great week for the person they would host?

While hosting a child from New York City may not be the match for you, there exists just the right formal volunteer opportunity, no matter how young or old you are, whether you're single or married, whether you make lots of money or very little money. Each of us has time to give and can offer our hearts and our unique talents. And as I have seen in countless cases, and through my own experiences, giving time is as valuable—sometimes more so—than writing a check.

Giving Time is Philanthropy

When I started in the field of philanthropy, an expert in the philanthropic sector said to me, "Giving time is nice, but giving money is generous."

Back in my early twenties, feeling insecure about how little money I made and had, I might have agreed with this statement. For years, I undervalued the contributions of time I made. When I didn't have money to give beyond $25, I gave my time. And though I followed in a long line of women who gave their time, I apologized for this contribution. "I don't have money to give, but I can give my time." I actually apologized for giving my time! Silly me. I allowed my time contribution to feel like it took a backseat to money contributions.

Like my shift in naming who could be a philanthropist, I experienced a shift in understanding the power and impact of giving time. What I learned: giving time is philanthropic. If anyone tells you differently, you tell them to give me a call. How do I know this for sure? Because of a man named Moose.

When I was twenty-two, I moved from Massachusetts to Seattle, Washington. Once I settled into my apartment and job, I started looking for volunteer opportunities. As someone who grew up having her mom plop her down in free public libraries and simply say, "Read," reading became a ridiculously enormous passion. I will read any novel. I will read the front, back, sides, and flaps of a Cheerios box. I will read pamphlets on root canals, scuba vacations, and car maintenance. If I'm ever sitting behind you on a train or bus and you feel me looking in your direction, I am likely trying to read the back cover of your magazine or the left side of your opened newspaper. (My apologies in advance.)

Given my passion and joy for reading, I knew I could give my all to literacy. Long before the internet produced results in seconds, I leaned on libraries and community colleges to guide me toward volunteer opportunities. It turned out that Seattle Central Community College was helping adults attain their GEDs, the equivalent of a high school diploma, and they were looking for volunteers. I signed up. In a short time, I gained my certification as an adult literacy tutor.

My first student was a man named Moose. At six feet tall, Moose towered over me. Born and raised in Washington State, he worked in an auto body shop. My stepdad had worked in an auto body shop and was a used car dealer, so Moose and I talked cars. We talked about our dream cars and the beauty of the practical Honda.

When we first met, Moose was shy. He walked in the room quietly, sat quietly, spoke quietly. I asked him why he had signed up for the reading comprehension class. He told me he was working to get his GED, having dropped out of school in fourth grade to help his family make ends meet. Moose's father had died when he was in fourth grade. Mine had, too. His father had been the breadwinner for his family, and to keep things going, Moose needed to drop out of school and work on the farm. Moose started working on the farm at the age of nine and continued until he was twenty-two. After his mom died, he sold the farm for a meager profit and got into auto body.

Talking to Moose, I realized how but for the grace of one circumstance, he and I could have traded places. My father died, but my mom remarried. Together, their full-time jobs helped keep me and my sisters going. I didn't have to drop out of school. I learned to read, which got me through middle school, high school, and on to college. If there hadn't been two incomes, I don't know where I would be today. Because of a single circumstance, Moose and I were led on different paths, but he and I were very much alike.

When I asked what prompted him now, at this age (he was thirty-five), to pursue his GED, Moose said he wanted to be able to read the paperwork he asked his customers to read and sign. That, and he wanted to read the newspaper.

I asked Moose how he knew how to fix cars when he couldn't read the manuals. He said that when he started at the auto body shop, he followed other guys around to learn the ropes. He said he watched what they did, listened as they read from manuals, and memorized everything. *He memorized everything.* Moose had the most extraordinary memory of anyone I had ever met. To this day, I've never met someone with a memory like his. "I had to," he said. "I couldn't tell people I couldn't read, so I memorized every nut and bolt. I memorized every word I heard."

But because he couldn't read, Moose didn't think he was smart. So we read. We read about sailboats, dinosaurs, and baseball. Using the instructor's book, I paused at the recommended places and asked him questions: what do you think the author was trying to convey when ...? Together, we sounded out words. I shared tips and tricks for pronunciation, use of past imperfect, and breaking down words into parts to figure out the definition. Moose was a natural learner. He absorbed every lesson like a sponge.

I remember our third lesson when, after covering some of the fundamentals, we read the first story in the reading comprehension book. Moose was nervous. I told him we'd take it one word and one sentence at a time. We sounded out the words that made up the story of a sailboat that got too big for its britches and sailed itself into the ocean. The sailboat had had enough of limitations and watching schooners go past him. He was going to show everyone what he was made of. Of course, the sailboat went out too far into the ocean and found himself riding waves bigger than he could handle. I don't remember how the story ended or its intended reading comprehension message, but I do remember that Moose read the story, with little help from me. At the end of it, I had my idea of what I thought the author was trying to convey: Life is the ocean; we are the sailboat. We have to know ourselves, pace ourselves, not get ahead of ourselves.

I asked Moose what he thought. He said he thought the sailboat was someone's soul and that no matter what anyone says, you can't keep a soul from seeking out bigger things, even if those things are scary.

Five months later, Moose completed his coursework. We volunteer instructors weren't allowed to read the students' critiques of us, but we were given advice and guidance by the staff who ran the program. I got a lot of great feedback from the directors, including my strengths and areas of improvement. After rating my performance, one of the directors said there was one thing in Moose's critique he wanted to share with me. It read: *Kathy made me feel smart.*

I did no such thing. I just was able to give my time to unleash his talents.

From this time as an adult literacy tutor, I learned about the power of giving time. Moose was gainfully employed. In fact, he earned more at his job than I did at mine. Moose did not need money from me; he needed my time to help him gain a skill I had been fortunate enough to gain early on in life. From there, new doors and new opportunities would open up for him.

Money isn't the sole solution. I thank and honor the donors who funded the adult literacy tutor program, and I hope they feel we volunteers did justice with their contributions. The further combination of time and treasure absolutely made a difference for Moose, and it helped me feel the absolute joy of giving time.

You, too, can have or continue to have meaningful and powerful experiences in giving your time. One way to ensure that the experience is fulfilling is to avoid burnout.

How to Give Your Time without Wearing Yourself Out

Giving your time can be overwhelming, and when a project needs lots of help, it can suck the volunteer life out of you. This quickly and easily causes burnout and will have you running for the hills. The answer to avoiding burnout is to be as wise with giving your time as you are with giving your money. Nancy found this out the hard way.

Nancy

When Nancy was asked to chair the auction committee for her children's school, she was more than happy to oblige. She had two children in the school system, and she wanted to give back to the school and to be a role model of volunteering for her kids. The first and second years of chairing the auction were great. Nancy did everything. She approached local businesses to get donated auction items, managed the volunteers who tagged the items, created the auction catalog, and oversaw logistics on the day of the auction. After the event, she hosted a volunteer thank-you party, wrote handwritten thank-you notes to the auction donors, and made a list of everything that worked and didn't work to help the next year's committee. Even though the volunteering took a lot of her time in those first two years, Nancy loved it. She felt she was investing in something that was meaningful to her children and her friend's children while helping the school raise much-needed funds.

However, by the third and fourth years, Nancy was overwhelmed and drained by the event. She felt it was consuming more time than she had to give. Her children were getting older, their schedules busier. The parents at the school called Nancy "Auction Empress" and showered her with comments about how great she was and how no one could do it as well. The result? No one took the lead on any of the auction needs because they thought Nancy could handle anything.

The *aha* moment for Nancy came when she realized that during auction season, she was spending more time in her home office than with her kids when they were home. "It was crazy. I was doing this to benefit my kids, but I was spending less and less time with them."

Nancy's lessons about this volunteer experience were about pacing herself and only giving as much time as she could. "I was happy to be the chair for a year but should have passed the baton after that. I would be there for the next chair but as an assistant, not as a leader."

She didn't want to disappoint anyone, so she kept saying yes even though she wanted to say no. Eventually, she felt burnt out and resentful. She stopped having a meaningful experience and felt like she needed a hiatus from volunteering.

Though I knew she wanted to run—not walk—from every committee within ten feet of her, I suggested Nancy do two things: One, vow to never be an empress of anything again. Delegating equals good. Overdoing it equals not good. Two, create a time budget. With a time budget, you figure out how many hours you have to give, and those are the hours you give. Just like budgeting money keeps you from draining your bank account down to zero, creating a time budget keeps you from draining your emotional resources down to a puddle of tired.

Creating a time budget is a quick and simple exercise. After Nancy took an inventory of her week (work, the kids, time for exercise, making dinner, movies, time with friends) and multiplied this times four weeks, she determined how many hours were filled during the month and how many—realistically—remained. Nancy learned she had two to three hours per week that she could give without burning out. Some months she could do more, while others she might not be able to give at all. However, what worked for Nancy was realizing she could contribute about a day to a day and a half per month, or twelve to eighteen days per year. This was a great starting point for her.

Armed with new knowledge about her time availability, Nancy went to the school and told the auction committee she could give a day a month. She asked if they could tell her their biggest needs, and she learned they needed help with organizing past fundraising files and with writing notes to donors. She agreed to volunteer a six-hour day per month to help meet these goals. For Nancy, who loves organizing and paperwork, this became a fulfilling formal volunteer experience. She had a task. She completed it. The school knew what could be expected from her. For other tasks, they secured volunteers, using Nancy's time budget as a model for recruiting.

Today, Nancy is not burned out with giving her time. And, because she feels fulfilled by her giving, she has added an extra day per month for the school. She feels her time and her talents are appreciated and respected, and she gets the time she needs and wants with her children. Nancy achieved joy again in giving her time.

For you, what will it mean to give your time? Have you given informally and want to become a formal volunteer? Or, maybe you've given formally and you want to start practicing generous acts of informal giving? What's important to answer is: What will be fulfilling to you? What will have you feeling that your time was well spent? What types of activities are you clear won't be fulfilling for you?

Having been a rabid volunteer activist in my high school and college years, I had thought then that giving time equaled total and utter exhaustion. I thought that unless I crawled into bed wondering what year it was, I hadn't really fought for the cause—I hadn't really given my all. I had given so much time that once a friend said, "Kathy, when I think of you, I think of Chronic Fatigue Syndrome." In college, I was the walking example of burning the candle at both ends. *How can I sleep or eat or shower*, I thought, *when there is so much that needs to be done?*

Making a change to a smarter use of my time happened when I recognized that I was becoming ineffective. Though I showed up for all my volunteer shifts, I lacked the enthusiasm and vigor needed to champion good work. The causes I cared about needed more and deserved better than the young woman who subsisted on black coffee and chocolate-covered peanuts. While I loved the work I was involved in, I often felt drained. I eventually became burned out and needed to take a reprieve. I didn't know that giving time didn't mean complete self-sacrifice to the point of blurry red eyes, wobbly legs, and dehydration.

Creating a time plan provided me with the structure and tools to know my limits, to be effective, and to feel fulfilled in giving my time. It was just after college that I created my first time-giving plan. When I aligned it with my vision and laid out what would fulfill me, that's when I began working with Moose and staffed a homeless women's shelter affiliated with the university where I worked. In these positions I was hands-on, effective, and making a difference. Plus, I was able to give up coffee and Visine.

As I've gotten older, I've revised how and in what ways I give my time. Some days it's still hard to say no, especially if I am jazzed by the volunteer opportunity. On those days, I tell myself, "Not now but soon!" That's an acceptable answer.

I, like you, want to be effective and to stay for the long haul. Creating a time budget, like Nancy did, will help you achieve this goal.

How then, can you be effective if you already have a full plate—if you look at your life and say, "Let's see, I can find about twelve minutes next Tuesday to help"? Here's how Doug figured out how to make giving his time work for him, even in a time-strapped life.

Doug

Doug is twenty-five years old and has been married less than a year. He holds down two jobs and takes a night class every semester, beginning his days at 5 AM and ending them at 11 PM. He takes time off on Sundays to spend with his spouse, rest and recuperate, and prepare himself for another back-to-back week.

What if you, like Doug, worked two jobs, took classes toward your degree, and were married or divorced with children? How would you give your time if you had so little to spare? Would you forego volunteering altogether?

Giving back is important to Doug. He generously contributes 8 percent of his total earnings to his extended family and to local nonprofits helping those in need.

Growing up, Doug went to a community center three days a week after school. He swam, played baseball, and worked on his homework until his mother picked him up. He fondly remembers the staff and coaches who were there for him. They tutored Doug, taught him to excel in sports, and built his confidence. His plan had always been to volunteer as a tutor or coach at a community center, but his family members told him he had too much going on already. He was burning the candle at both ends, they said.

But, Doug felt strongly about giving his time. He felt if he didn't find a way to make it work then, he would always find a reason why he couldn't fit it into this life. So he started by looking at how he spent his days: work, school, and family. When he broke down how he spent his time, he realized that he could possibly support a fellow student in his business finance class. He was doing well in the class. Because of his proficiency, he could be a guide to someone who might be having a difficult time.

He approached the instructor and offered to tutor a student for two hours after class each week. The professor told him he would survey the class to see if there were any takers. While none of the students took him up on the offer, the instructor remembered a student who wanted to take the class but felt the subject matter was too tough for him. He had asked the professor if he could audit the class and had come twice, but he felt intimidated and wasn't sure he'd return. The instructor asked Doug if he'd be interested in working with this student to help ready him for the class the following semester. Doug did just that.

For eight weeks, Doug worked with Jim for two hours after class. While Doug completed the homework, he walked Jim through his thinking. He shared which business finance practices he applied to a problem and why, how he solved the problem of the entrepreneur who couldn't maintain steady cash flow, and the ins and outs of a profit-and-loss sheet.

Eight weeks of weekly two-hour tutoring sessions was just the support Jim needed to enroll in the class the following semester. A year later, Jim emailed Doug to share that he had passed the class and was ready to take level two of the class. He also wrote that he had offered to volunteer for a student in need two hours after every class at the same location they had met for their tutoring sessions.

Though Doug's schedule was packed, he found a way to give back, working within the parameters of his own life. He leaned on his talents to guide him and worked with the time he had available. While he still plans to become a coach at a local YMCA or a Boys and Girls Club, twice a year he will continue to tutor a student in business finance. Of the experience, Doug said that tutoring actually improved his own learning capacity because he had to see his class topic through the lens of someone else, figuring out how concepts made sense from multiple points of view. He also said that he knows he wouldn't be where he is without the tutors and coaches from the community center. He now knows why they did it and why they kept coming back week after week and year after year.

As with Nancy and Doug, the key to finding ways to give your time is enjoying the time you are contributing. You must enjoy your volunteer activities in order to keep coming back and to keep making a difference. If you say yes to a task because no one else will do it or because you feel you should, you are not giving your time in the smartest or most effective way. For the optimal volunteer experience, one that is gratifying and rewarding, choose the cause and opportunituy that is right for you.

While I feel proud of the checks I have written, my warmest experiences are with the people I have met and worked with while giving my time. From the women in the former Yugoslavia, who showed me what it meant to stand up for what you believe in, to Moose, who taught me the meaning of courage and resolve, these people helped me learn that giving your time unleashes a generosity you did not know you had.

Give your time, formally and informally. Give it to the causes you care about most. Get to know the people behind the cause. Set limits. Feel the joy of volunteering and watch what you will help create. Unless you give more time than you have or want to, giving your time is not something you regret.

6
How Much Can You Contribute?
Creating Your Giving Formula

*I*n this chapter, you are going to add a lot of muscle to your Generosity Plan. You will create the right giving amount for your budget and your life for the short-term and long-term and, in doing so, transform your values and hopes into action.

Because our wallets can be both a source of celebration and stress, you'll look at your attitudes about money and learn how these feelings impact how much money you have given to your favorite cause in the past and in the present. You'll then look more closely at this giving and make a determination if this amount is reflective of your capacity and your hopes for your charitable life.

Having taken these important steps, you'll determine just the right amount of your finances to share and will learn how to easily and seamlessly make these contributions, with minimum over-whelm and maximum joy.

Lastly, we'll explore giving in uncertain financial times, arming you with the tools you need to give to your capacity and desire, no matter the size of your wallet or the state of the economy.

Trust me when I share that if you've not written capacity checks before, you're going to love it. It's a lot more fun than writing checks to your landlord or mortgage company. If you've written checks before that are your capacity, this section will serve as an important audit to keep you on track and moving forward.

Comparing What You Give to the Average Giving

On average, individuals and families in the United States give about 3.2 percent of their income to charitable organizations.[20] For some, this number is a little lower. For others, much higher.

Think of what you make monthly or annually. Now calculate 3.2 percent of this total. What is that number? Here is an example: If you make $42,000 a year, 3.2 percent of that is $1,244 per year, or $112 per month, or $28 per week. If you made and donated these amounts, you would be on average with most families in the United States.

When you calculated 3.2 percent of your earnings, what did you think of the resulting number? Was it less than you thought? More? Did it seem impossible to think of giving that amount to charity in consideration of your current financial obligations? When you broke it down to a per-week number, did that seem more achievable?

Now that you know what the U.S. average is, look at what you are currently contributing. You don't need to have an exact number, just a ballpark. If you have last year's tax returns and on those you listed your charitable contributions, pull out the returns and jot down the number. If, however, you don't have returns or receipts from charitable groups, you can make a list of groups you know you've written checks to. Do you have an organization you normally give to once or more per year? Do you give to your college? Church? Mosque? Temple? Are you part of a monthly pledge program in which your credit card is charged $25 each month? Have you recently made a gift in response to an urgent need, such as a natural disaster? Have you made a gift to someone involved in a bike-a-thon? Have you recently bought Girl Scout Cookies or raffle tickets? Did you give money to a family member in need?

Take the amounts—no matter their size—and add them up. This is how much you gave in total in the last year. Now that you have this number, let's calculate your current charitable giving as a percentage. For example, if your giving totaled $250 and last year you earned $30,000, then your charitable giving percentage is less than 1 percent.

Looking at our giving from a percentage perspective versus how many dollars we gave is helpful in determining how much we can contribute for two reasons: First, if you make $30,000 a year and I were to ask you for $250 for a cause you care about, you may think, *That's a lot of money. I don't have that much money to give.* You may even be a little shocked that I am asking for that amount. If, however, I asked if you would like to commit to giving less than one percent of your annual salary to your favorite cause, you may feel more comfortable weighing that possibility.

Second, creating your giving budget based on percentages and not dollar amount is a smart and empowering way to give. If you decide you want to give 5 percent of your wages or salary to charitable efforts, you are stating that you want philanthropy to occupy 5 percent of your total budget. This is an intentional decision that is rooted in your values. A certain percentage of your money goes to a roof over your head, food, fuel, children, fun. Add into your pie a generosity designation that best reflects the place that contributing to the greater good occupies in your life, or that you would like it to occupy. This approach removes the stress that can be associated with finding money to share and ensures that you are putting your money where your values live.

Jeff

As a salesman, Jeff went years making a base salary while the rest of his earnings were commission based. He spent these years proving himself. He knocked on countless doors, made cold call after cold call. Mostly, he made ends meet with a few bonuses here and there. Through it all, he loved sales. And he stuck it out, knowing that one day he would turn the corner and get some of the bigger fish clients.

That day came five years ago, when Jeff hit a career high. With it came bigger checks and bigger bonuses. He bought himself a few nice things he had dreamed of owning back when he was barely making rent on his apartment and driving a run-down car.

When he shared with a friend his good fortune and his enthusiasm about his future with the company, his friend told him he should think about sharing some of his fortune with a charity. His friend had been involved in a charity that provided scholarships to terminally ill children to attend summer camp. Jeff wanted to know more, so his friend sent him brochures about the camp. At first glance, he thought to sponsor one scholarship in the amount of $2,500. Then, after talking to his friend and hearing his friend say that sponsoring two is better than one, he decided to match his friend's giving by paying for two children to attend the camp. Jeff sent $5,000 and was thrilled. He told me it was as fun—well, almost as fun—as paying off his old debts.

While Jeff came to his donation number with a dollar amount initially, he was happy when he realized that $5,000 represented 5 percent of his earnings from that year. For Jeff, 5 percent felt like a good starting point and a sustainable amount for his generosity. After making the first gift, he decided that if children's lives were enriched as a result of his contribution, he would continue to be involved at this level.

Then as life does, it showed up on its own terms. Jeff's company filed for bankruptcy, and he and his coworkers all lost their jobs. Jeff was anxious and scared, but he began doing what he needed to do to find a new job. It took a few months—and some draining of his retirement account to pay the bills—but he was successful in finding a new position. Although it wasn't the high-level position he had just been laid off from, it wasn't entry level either. After reworking his budget for his adjusted salary, Jeff was concerned that he could no longer afford the $5,000 donation to the summer camp, and he was upset. He had grown to love the camp and was worried he'd be letting the kids down.

What we talked about was Jeff letting go of the dollar amount he could afford and instead focus on the commitment to give 5 percent of his earnings to the summer camp. I shared with him that so often when we lose income, we tend to cut giving completely, primarily because we feel we can't do what we once did or we're worried we'll go without.

For Jeff, giving to the summer camp made him feel like his work and his efforts were making a difference for kids in need. To let go of that because of reduced income would not serve his vision or his hopes for young people. To maintain his commitment to generosity that he made prior to losing his job, Jeff decided to continue giving to the summer camp at 5 percent. While this new 5 percent translated to $1,500 instead of $5,000, it represented Jeff's deep personal commitment to living a generous life and to supporting children living with terminal illness.

Last year, when Jeff made his $1,500 gift, he made a plan to reach out to two colleagues and invite them to match at the same level. They did. Because of Jeff, $4,500 was sent to the camp and two new friends were introduced to the joy of supporting these children.

I share this approach because it has worked for so many, including me. For some years, I was able to give away a good amount of money to my favorite social change efforts. Then in the past few years as I worked to grow my business, I, like many other entrepreneurs, borrowed, borrowed, and borrowed to pay for start-up costs. Because of these debts, I wasn't able to give at the same dollar level. I did, however, maintain the same percentage. Though my contribution amount changed, my commitment did not. I also supplemented my financial gifts by giving my time and talents at an accelerated level. To ensure I was giving to my full generosity capacity, for every five hours of paid work, I gave away one hour of professional consulting. While it wasn't the check size I once wrote, the commitment remained the same.

To feel good how about how much you contribute—be it $1 per month or $100,000 per year—commit to a percentage of your earnings going to your hope for the world. I can almost guarantee you'll practically be knocking on Bill Gates's door, asking him if he feels as good as you do.

In your Generosity Journal, revisit your percentage from the exercises above. When you learned your number, what did you think of it? Is it reflective of the portion of your budget you want to allocate to generosity? Is it just about right? Is it lower than you thought? Would you like it to be more but you can't really see how you could increase it, given debts or other obligations? For now, simply write down your giving percentage and any initial thoughts that emerge. Later in the chapter, we'll come back to it and help you land on the percentage that works for your life, your giving roots, your vision, and your voice. Until then, let's explore how you think about money. Once you know the *how*, you will be better equipped to know *how much* is right for you to share.

Whether you are rich, middle class, or low-income, or you feel rich, middle class, or low-income, you very likely have feelings about money—very strong feelings. If you are to feel empowered by your financial giving and powerful each time you write a check, you have to first take a look at how you feel about money in general and your own personal money. This section won't examine how you came to learn about money, your first impressions of it, whether the first money you held in your hands was earned or a gift. The following exercises and stories will help you to gain insight into your attitudes about money and its purpose. From here, you will be better ready to unlock your true giving capacity and, in doing so, to round out your time, treasure, and talent plan.

When I Think About Money . . .

Money is one loaded word. Let's see if we can take it down a notch.

Since we've looked at the definitions of *philanthropy*, *time*, *treasure*, *talent*, *stand*, and *charity*, let's not leave out *money*. Before we go to Merriam-Webster's dictionary, take a moment to jot down what you think the definition of money is. Or if you are completing these exercises with family, friends, or a small group, talk your answers out.

What is money? What is the purpose of money?

Let's start with the real definition of money. Webster's defines money as "something generally accepted as a medium of exchange, a measure of value, or a means of payment."

These are fairly simple and straightforward concepts. They work in the barter system—the equal exchange of goods—as well as in the system of currency. Money, it seems, exists to ensure that exchange is fair, based on values, and easy. However, it's not likely that the words you used to describe money and its purpose included: *fair, based on values*, and *easy*.

How did you define money and its purpose? Were your definitions loaded with emotion (*money is the bane of my existence*)? Were your definitions factual or clear-cut (*money is currency*)?

Think about how you defined it. Now ask yourself how these feelings about money and its purpose impact how you share your money with a good cause. In other words, consider if there are any emotional or logical reasons that are preventing you from moving forward with your plan. And while you as an individual might have certain beliefs about money, it's also important to consider how your beliefs interact with those of your spouse, partner, or family as a group. Each perspective contributes to the overall Generosity Plan in action. A married couple I once worked with, Rich and Marlene, did this, and they were surprised by what they found.

Rich and Marlene

Rich had a successful job in manufacturing, complete with a good salary and benefits. Marlene worked part-time as a cosmetics representative. Their expenses included one child, a mortgage, two car payments, a few credit cards, their son's college tuition, and the regular costs of living.

Rich's annual income was $72,000, and Marlene's was $23,000, making their total income $95,000 per year.

Rich and Marlene followed the exercises above and found that if they were to give away 3.2 percent of their annual salary—the U.S. average—that would translate to $3,040 per year. They made a note of this in their Generosity Journal.

They then reviewed their giving from the previous year: They gave money to both their colleges, their church, and a fundraising athletic event their son participated in. Total giving from the year prior: $2,900, just slightly below the national average. Then they broke down $2,900 into month and week figures. Per month, their charitable giving was $241. Per week: $60.

Next they looked at how they defined money—what they saw its purpose to be and how these ideas impacted their giving. For Rich, money was "currency you earn to make a good life," and its purpose was "to make life easier and more enjoyable." Marlene said that the definition of money was something that allows you to pay for what you need and to enjoy what life has to offer. She stated its purpose as helping you to have the life you hope for, to support your child, and to support your community.

As they reviewed their percentage of giving, Marlene felt they weren't giving enough. She said that both she and Rich easily spend $60 per week on "things we don't necessarily need or maybe even want" but just pick up along the way. She said she'd like to double their current giving of $60 a week to $120 per week. She thought that while it would require a little more attention, it wouldn't actually be stressful on their budget. The reason for increasing her giving percentage from 3 percent to 6 percent? "Part of the purpose of money—to me—is to support others, not just to support me and my own."

Rich had a different take. Because he saw money as something to make life easier and more enjoyable, he didn't feel as pressured to give more than 3 percent to his church and school. Rich felt that by paying federal and state taxes and paying for his son's life until he finished college, he was meeting his social obligation. However, Rich did feel that maybe he and Marlene spent a little "haphazardly." He said he could certainly see them getting smarter about their spending, and he would not be averse to taking what could be "money we blow through" and setting it aside for charity. "It's not like we'd miss that money, and if it can be put to use to help our church's outreach efforts to those in need, that would be a good thing."

Rich and Marlene's story is important for several reasons. First, while they were sharing their money with the causes they cared about, they hadn't had a discussion about how much. They just wrote checks, which both of them described as "fine but not really fulfilling." Second, it did not take long to look at their percentage and to answer the questions about money and its purpose. They learned that they shared similar notions about money and money's role, but that their opinions diverged when it came to sharing personal money outside of the family. Lastly, when they realized that it certainly wouldn't upset them to give more and that in fact they could feel more empowered about their giving—especially if they spent less recklessly—they felt good about the decision to increase their giving.

The point here is that Rich and Marlene made an intentional decision about how much to give. They looked at their personal budget and felt that giving 5 percent instead of 3 percent would be a more accurate reflection of their personal commitment to helping out and making a difference. They shared that after their son had graduated and landed on his feet, they could revisit their 5 percent commitment and possibly increase their giving percentage. Their agreement: "To be committed to our charities of choice and at least contribute 5 percent of what we make, knowing that we could increase to 7 or even 10 percent when our expenses decrease."

What about for you? Did you like your percentage? Would you want to change it? What percentage would feel empowering to you?

The exercises around creating your giving budget are similar to thinking about giving your time. If *person A* feels pressed for time and doesn't feel she has one extra minute in the day to breathe, she won't likely think about volunteering five hours per month at the local library. Or, if *person A* is already volunteering, she might find that she is being drained by this giving of time because she feels she has no time for herself.

Alternately, if *person B* feels that he has a good handle on his time, that he has and follows a time budget that helps him meet obligations to family, friends, work, and self, then he might feel he has five hours per month to help a stranger in need.

Both *person A* and *person B* may in fact have five hours per month to give to volunteering. What distinguishes their giving of time is how they feel about the time they have. When it comes to time, do they feel it is well managed, or do they constantly feel rushed and stressed out? Do they feel they take the time, even if it's fifteen minutes a day, to care for themselves? Or do they feel the only time they get is late at night when they're already exhausted and can't imagine having any time to give?

What holds true for perceptions and realities about time holds true for money. While you may be able to give 3 or 5 or 10 percent of your annual income to your favorite cause, if you feel you don't have enough, or you're worried about your future, you may be giving less than your true giving capacity. On the other hand, if you feel more calm and confident about your money and have a budget that includes a line item for generosity, you're more likely to give to your capacity.

As you create the right percentage for you—just as Rich, Marlene, and Jeff did—continue to work on knowing how you see money. Do you see how supporting your favorite cause can make opportunities available (*if I'm more organized with my time and more cautious with my money, I can make a real difference*)? Or do you see only hurdles when it comes to getting involved (*I'm already strapped for cash and deep in debt, and can't imagine finding even an extra dollar to give*)?

There's a difference between having absolutely no more to give—you've looked at your budget and found your percentage of giving is at its maximum—and not really knowing and staying stuck in the same mantra of "I have no money."

How do you profile when it comes to seeing possibility versus seeing barriers? Do you see hurdles or opportunities? For example, if you're worried about making ends meet, this could impact your giving money in one of two ways: you either feel you need to hold on to as much money as you can, or you give away what you can because you know others are worse off than you. Or if you're worried about paying for your children's education, you may give nothing financially until school is complete, or you may feel compelled to support those in need and then encourage your kids to apply for scholarships or summer jobs to help them pay for school. If you're retired and feel you are living on a comfortable budget, you may hold back some in case your retirement account shrinks, or you might feel this is the time in your life you waited for so you could give back and make a difference.

The bottom line is how you think about money—having too little, just enough, or too much—will directly impact what you think you can give and how you determine what you can afford to give. By knowing your real capacity, you will feel more fulfilled with each check you write, knowing that you are truly "doing what you can, with what you have, where you are." No more, no less.

How to Budget Generosity

Back in chapter 3, we looked at creating a time budget. No matter your income, you very likely have a financial budget that you follow. Some months you may follow that budget closely and to the penny. Other months, you may be more liberal with spending. Mostly, though, you likely have a good sense of your cost of living.

When we look at our expenses—mortgage, cell phone, gasoline, food—we rarely think about those costs as once-a-year events. For mortgages and credit cards, we pay our balances once a month. For consumable costs like food, fuel, and that run to Starbucks, our expenditures are weekly or even daily.

However, when we think about giving to the causes we care about most, we tend to write checks at the end of the year or when asked by an annual fund or a letter in the mail. We sometimes hold on to letters until we have enough money to give what we hoped and planned to give.

While some can give at the end of the year—from assets, birthday money, the sale of a business or property, a bonus from work—for many, giving is less of a financial burden when it becomes a monthly activity. If we wait until the year-end to think about giving away the percentage we've assigned to generosity, we may experience some stress and anxiety. We also may not have the amount we had planned for.

If you don't need to budget giving because you have the resources to write your charitable checks, you likely won't need the following section. If, however, you wouldn't be able to come up with your charitable giving in one fell swoop, this next section will help you budget your giving.

A Look at the Numbers

If you have already decided the percentage of your wages or salary you'd like to give, you'll now get to see how that breaks down into concrete amounts. If you haven't yet decided on your percentage, you'll be able to see the translated dollar amounts. Either way, this section is designed to help you make giving affordable:

Salary/year	1 percent	3 percent	5 percent	8 percent	10 percent
$25,000	$250	$750	$1,250	$2,000	$2,500
$40,000	$400	$1,200	$2,000	$3,200	$4,000
$50,000	$500	$1,500	$2,500	$4,000	$5,000
$70,000	$700	$2,100	$3,500	$5,600	$7,000
$80,000	$800	$2,400	$4,000	$6,400	$8,000

Let's say your take-home pay is $25,000 a year and you'd like to aim for your percentage of giving to be 3 percent. This would break down to $750 per year, $62 per month, or $15.50 a week.

Can you envision affording $15.50 a week? If not today, what steps could you take to be able to afford this amount? Would creating a budget and sticking to it be enough? Or putting $2 or $3 a day in a coffee can marked "Generosity"? How about once you pay off a credit card, putting that monthly payment aside for generosity? If you couldn't afford $15.50 a week right now, what could you afford? Could you afford $30.00 a month, or $7.50 a week?

Remember from chapter 1, we defined *generosity* as a "habit of giving." It doesn't matter where your starting point is with your financial generosity, you must start somewhere. Start where you are. You will be amazed and surprised how much you have to give when you start where you are.

When you budget generosity, you flex your giving muscle and you make financial generosity more achievable. In the beginning, it may be a struggle to figure out how to make it work. Don't worry. You'll get it quickly. Take the time to get accustomed to having and living a generosity budget.

Erika

Growing up, Erika didn't learn how to budget from her parents. They just didn't talk about money with Erika or her brother. Both parents worked, bills were paid on time, and the family took a one-week family vacation every year, usually within driving distance of where they lived. Erika and her brother always had clothes for back-to-school time, books and supplies, and presents at Christmas.

In the summers they played outside with their friends, climbing trees, playing Wiffle Ball, and swimming in the lake down the street. They didn't go away to camp or take piano or skiing lessons. They knew of kids who did this, but Erika never felt they were missing out. She always felt safe and comfortable and that they had a good childhood.

She knew her parents gave back to their church but wasn't sure how much. One day, Erika heard her dad say to her mom that once they'd paid everything they needed to pay and put aside money for spending, whatever was leftover could go to their church. This made sense to Erika: you take care of your responsibilities and needs, and then you give what you can from what's leftover.

In high school, Erika got involved with her school's environmental club, and she was passionate about it. While some people thought this was a phase for Erika, it was not. Erika went on to college for environmental studies, and when she graduated, she got a job working for an environmental rights organization.

As a young adult, Erika earns $28,000 per year. Like her parents before her, Erika lives within her means. However, her job is in a city, and living in a city costs more than living in the rural area where she grew up.

As a result, Erika often experiences difficulties budgeting her money. She doesn't overspend, but even so, with the cost of living in the city, she tends to run out of money a few days before her next paycheck. She often finds herself needing to use her overdraft account for groceries and spending money. She thought if she paid a little more attention to her spending, she could avoid running out of money, so she tried a few approaches—creating a life budget, writing down every purchase she made with cash or her debit card, evaluating her spending to see where she could cut back. She was able to do these activities for a week or so but eventually grew bored and went back to spending as she had, knowing she had the overdraft account as a cushion.

For Erika, the disappointment around running out of money before her next paycheck wasn't the stress of using her overdraft. She knew that leaning on the overdraft wasn't ideal, but she always paid it back within seventy-two hours and it didn't incur more than $25 in fees. The disappointment around not having a budget that worked was that she didn't have money left to fund her social change work.

She loves the nonprofit where she works and wants to make a financial contribution back to the organization. Since she witnesses firsthand the impact this organization has on protecting the environment, this is the place where she wanted to contribute her time, talents, and treasure.

Each pay period, Erika plans to write a check to the organization totaling 5 percent of that paycheck amount. However, by the time she catches up from her prior deficit, pays her bills, and puts aside spending money, she usually has no money left over. Every time she looks at the zero balance on the paper, she promises herself that she will spend less in the coming two weeks. She promises that the next paycheck will be different. But Erika still hasn't been able to write a check to the organization. She feels that in order for her Generosity Plan to work, she has to have the treasure piece working as well as the time and talent piece.

So she decided to create a giving budget. And when Erika set out to do so, her hope was that it would serve as the impetus to create and live by a personal life budget. Because giving to environmental groups is important to Erika, she feels this passion could help her develop a discipline around budgeting. Trying to create a budget based on paying off student loans and credit card debt, or not using her checking account's overdraft, is clearly not enough of a motivator for Erika. She recognizes that in order for a budget to work, it has to work for her. In short, her budget has to serve her values, rather than her values trying to play catch-up to her spending.

Erika chose 5 percent to donate based on two primary factors: One, if she got smarter about spending, this would be an affordable and manageable amount. Two, she felt that anything under 5 percent didn't reflect her personal commitment to supporting environmental wellness.

Erika took home $1,077 every two weeks, and 5 percent is $54. Erika had to ask herself, *Can I really set aside $54 every two weeks to give back to my organization?* She looked closely at her bank statements with her friend Monica. While Erika made notes about how many times she used her debit card for coffee runs, movies, magazines, pizza deliveries, and dinners out, Monica made a list of fees that Erika was accruing. They then looked at the two lists. As Erika suspected, she was modest when it came to spending. Having grown up where summer play was filled with climbing trees, swimming in the local lake, and watching late-night movies with her friends, Erika wasn't used to spending a lot of money for leisure activities, even though many of her friends would spend $100–$200 a week on socializing. However, while her spending was less than her friends', it was actually more than she could afford. She wasn't sure how her colleagues from work could spend how they did, but she knew that if she wanted to give back, she would have to cut back on going out one night a week.

Reviewing the list proved to be illuminating and compelling for Erika. Each time Erika charged toward her overdraft, her bank charged her $20. After she figured out she was being charged $20 for any charge amount—be it a $2 iced tea or a $50 run to the grocery store—she began to withdraw a sum of cash, spend from that cash, and incur only one $20 charge. However, Monica calculated that in the last six-month period, Erika had used the overdraft eleven times.

Erika and Monica did the math: $20 x 11 = $220. Erika then divided $220 by $54, the amount she wanted to give to her nonprofit as part of her Generosity Plan. The divisible: 4.0. Erika realized that if she had not incurred bank fees over the last six months, she could already have made four times worth of financial giving to her charitable organization.

Erika then asked for Monica's help in seeing where she could cut back so that she wouldn't have to lean on the overdraft. First, she agreed not to use her debit card for a few months. She would take out cash from the ATM for a week and live on that. By living on cash, Erika spent less because she had less in her hands to spend. While she wasn't sure she could follow this plan to the tee, she agreed that her goal would be to avoid using the overdraft unless an emergency came up, such as a doctor's appointment not covered by insurance.

Within six months of starting her giving budget, Erika had gone from using her overdraft account eleven times to only two times. Before she started her plan, she hadn't realized how many bank fees she was paying. And while she tried to get a handle on it by putting budget first, Erika was more motivated by putting values and passion first, thereby finding the solution to her budgeting challenges.

Because she still had debts to pay and didn't want to fall behind, Erika committed to giving 4.5 percent, rather than 5 percent, of her earnings to her nonprofit. Her agreement with herself was that if she got a promotion within the organization, she would increase that giving by a full percentage point.

To keep to her plan, Erika starting writing out her check for her nonprofit at the same time she wrote out her rent, car payment, car insurance, and student loan checks. By doing this, Erika ensured that the amount that went to charity was not simply what was left over at the end of the month. Charity is now a key line item in Erika's budget; it's no longer in the leftover pile.

Taking a Percentage Leap!

Erika decided that she would take a full percentage point leap when she got a promotion. She knew that going to 5 or 5.5 percent before the promotion would be a strain on her and would take away the joy of giving her treasure. While she didn't want to give less than she could, she also didn't want to get ahead of herself. She knew that keeping a commitment works best if that commitment is achievable, workable, and sustainable, much like the values of her nonprofit. She felt that if it worked for the environmental rights movement, it could work for her.

How do you know when it's the right time to increase the percentage of your giving? Do you wait until you've paid off a debt? Should it be when you get a raise or promotion? What about if a family member left you a little money—should that be the moment that prompts you to increase your percentage?

Here's what I've learned: we increase our giving percentage when we feel dissatisfied about our current giving percentage and/or feel so passionate about our cause that we will work the numbers day and night to make an increase work.

When I learned about an organization providing shelter to chimpanzees who had been used in roadside entertainment venues, I knew I had to modify my spending to increase my gifts to them. I was so moved by the four women who ran the sanctuary, by their dedication to providing optimal care to the animals, and by the organization's passionate belief in the work that I was inspired to make my money work for my vision and my values. I found ways to contribute a few additional dollars here and there because the work motivated me beyond my own anxieties around having enough money.

Because I was moved by these women's efforts, I have found new ways to give. For example, the past few months, I have cashed in my credit card points for a dollar amount which is then sent to the sanctuary. While this averages around $100 a month, it adds up. In just a year, I will be able to give an additional $1,200. This is helping me to meet my percentage goal increases and is inviting me to be wise and creative when it comes to my spending.

For Judy, whom I met through a mutual friend, increasing her giving to her goal of 10 percent was proving to be a difficult challenge. She leaned on the tools of the Generosity Plan to help her find her way to her goal.

Judy

Judy is a quiet person who is fastidious about budgeting. She has never been late on a bill and, nine times out of ten, could give you her checking account balance to the penny. (As someone who is the anti-Judy when it comes to money and bills, I bow to her.)

A bookkeeper for more than forty years, Judy loves numbers. She loves seeing the numbers balance to zero because of a job well-done. She takes pride in her work and is comforted knowing that her bookkeeping skills helps her keep and maintain her commitment to her church.

Judy has always given 10 percent of her earnings to her church. Each week she writes out a check for a quarter of the amount owed for the month and drops it into the collection basket. She has done so for thirty-eight years.

Then, seven years ago, Judy's husband suffered an illness that had him hospitalized multiple times. There were expensive tests and medications not covered by insurance. Judy reworked her budget, cutting back in each area including donations to her church. After a lifetime of giving 10 percent, she needed to cut back to 4 percent. She went to her pastor, who, of course, was kind and understanding. He shared with Judy that she had already given so much material support to the church that she could take a hiatus from giving, but Judy still maintained her 4 percent. She felt the church had given her so much that she wanted to continue to support its good efforts. She also knew that during her husband's illness, she would need to lean on the church as never before.

A year after Judy's husband had become ill, he passed away. Having had no children, Judy felt lost and alone. She turned to her pastor, her congregation, and her women's group for comfort and support.

Within two years, Judy was feeling stronger and better. She increased her volunteering efforts in the church and even began to get involved in other community events. She also felt financially stable, as the life insurance from her husband's death paid his medical debts and funeral costs.

In reviewing her finances, Judy felt ready to return to 10 percent of her giving. In fact, she hoped to increase it to 12 percent. She felt as though the church community had gotten her through an extremely difficult period, and she wanted to give back and support them as they had supported her.

Even as someone who handled money matters extremely well, Judy was having a hard time figuring out how to get to 12 percent, or even back to 10 percent. Though her late husband's medical bills were paid off, the cost of living had increased in the past three years, and she was taking a new medication for her blood pressure that was not covered by her health insurance plan. The company she worked for was small and hadn't been in a position to give cost-of-living raises. In fact, Judy didn't make much more than when she started at the company eighteen years prior.

For Judy, going from giving 4 percent to 10 percent of her earnings, and eventually to giving 12 percent, was a financial leap. While necessity can help us scale back, reworking our budgets to open up more space for giving can be a challenge.

Judy's anxiety about going back to 10 percent as quickly as she could was to "make up for lost time." She felt such gratitude to the church and wanted to illustrate that through tithing. However, while she crunched the numbers, she realized that without a cost-of-living raise, leaping too quickly would be difficult to sustain.

Judy then leaned on the tools of the Generosity Plan program to help her find the right number and make peace with it. She looked back to her giving roots. She looked at how much time she had given to the church. She remembered the meetings she attended and helped facilitate. She recalled fifteen years earlier, when the church's bookkeeper left suddenly and she filled in for free until a replacement was hired. She thought about how she had helped to grow the women's group and how that group had raised money for the church and the soup kitchen.

She then attempted to calculate her total treasure contributions over the course of her thirty-eight years with the church. She stopped after twenty-five years, when she realized that she had given $30,000 to her church. When she saw this number, she laughed, smiled, and cried. She had often wondered if, when she and her husband took a vacation, they were spending too much on themselves. Realizing that she had given more than $30,000 in support of an institution that had done so much for others, Judy came to see how she had truly matched her money with her values.

Feeling this sense of connection and commitment, Judy felt less anxious about having to slowly and steadily build her giving back to 10 percent. She realized that her job where generosity was concerned was to give her treasure over the course of her life. Sometimes, that would be a little more; other times that would be a little less.

Slow and steady—she began to feel—truly *does* win the race. With this in mind, she went to her bosses and asked for a small raise, which she had never done before. She then increased her giving from 4 percent to 6 percent. Today, Judy gives 7 percent of her earnings to her church and plans to be back at 10 percent when she is sure she can sustain that level. She feels good about this percentage because she knows it is her capacity.

Ideas to Help You Meet Your Giving Goals

No matter how much you can give per month—$5 or $5,000—or how much you can give a year, you can always leverage your gift and your impact.

Here are tried and true ways to amplify your impact:

Lisa: Create an Informal 3 Percent and Growing Club

Because of her expenses—including two toddlers—Lisa determined she can afford to give 3 percent of her income to her favorite causes. However, her hope is to increase her giving over time from 3 percent to 5 percent. To motivate herself, her family, and her friends to do the same, Lisa launched an informal 3 Percent and Growing! club. Using an online mailing list, she and her friends share ways that they are getting closer to going from 3 percent to 4 percent to 5 percent. By sharing ideas about reducing expenses, such as putting spare dollars and coins in a coffee can, allocating a percentage of a company bonus to generosity, or going out to dinner one less time per month, Lisa and her family and friends are well on their way to reaching their 5 percent goals.

Jillian: Match Me

Like Jeff, Jillian invited friends and colleagues who shared her vision to match her giving. Her idea had a domino effect. New folks were brought in one at a time and, before she knew it, Jillian directly and indirectly brought in ten new supporters to her cause.

Nathan: Share What You Are Doing and Why

Every year, Nathan makes a top ten list of his favorite organizations and sends this as part of his holiday or end-of-year letter to friends and family. This helps get the word out and may just add another donor or two to the organization's family of givers. Nathan doesn't share the amount he gives, but he does share why he gives to each and why the organizations mean so much to him.

Jacki: Blog about Your Favorite Organizations

As a committed blogger, Jacki has a section on her site called "Open Your Purse." She writes about her favorite causes and organizations, creates links to their websites, and encourages readers to learn more.

Create Your Giving Formula

Take a few moments now to think about how much you would like to contribute this year to the causes you care about most. Remember to play with the numbers, move them around; you'll land on the right amount for you.

By yourself or with your family, friends, or a group, use the chart on page 119 to begin to calculate giving at 1 percent, 3 percent, 5 percent, 10 percent, or—if you're debt free and not a big spender—even more. If you make an hourly wage, calculate based on earnings per week or every two weeks.

What's truly affordable? What will be the right starting point for you? Would you like to grow your percentage over time? Would you like to put aside money every week? Every month? Do you have a bonus coming this year? Could you allocate a percentage of it now toward your total generosity goal?

What kind of support do you need from friends and family to hit your percentage goal (*remind me to save spare money in my Generosity jar!*)? Do you have a friend you can buddy with to meet your goals? If cash feels tight but you still want to hit a certain goal, can you fundraise for the balance?

You will feel powerful when you add a generosity line item to your life budget. Be proud of the amount you decide on. Don't go beyond a level that is manageable and achievable. By the same token, don't underestimate what you can give. When you begin regularly writing checks to the causes that are important to you, you will feel that you are the philanthropist the world has been waiting for. This is in you.

Generosity During Uncertain Financial Times

Countries face uncertain financial times. So do counties, cities, companies, nonprofits, households, individuals. What, then, does our financial giving look like during uncertain financial times? While many may be tempted to withdraw giving altogether, we can all take a lead from individuals like Jeff, who adjusted his giving to match his checking account rather than eliminating it when his financial picture changed.

By continuing to give his financial resources, Jeff discovered that each of us is a change agent no matter the size of our wallet. To be that change agent every day, we must do what we can, with what we have, where we are. If it's $1, so be it. Give it. The habit of giving—the act of living a generous life—will keep your heart strong and your soul connected no matter the pluses or minuses in your bank accounts.

Giving and generosity can help you live your values and, quite amazingly, can help you mange the stress.

Regina

When Regina's husband, Alex, lost his job as a corporate consultant, the family leaned on her income. However, as the months wore on, their accounts began to dwindle. They revisited their budget and cut where they could.

Six months into his unemployment, Alex realized that Regina was still giving a monthly gift to their community's senior center. Her husband said that while he cared about this center, they couldn't afford it. He said that for now, others would need to step up and fund the center; they just didn't have it in their budget. Regina pushed back, saying it was only $50 and it was important to do. Alex was angry and called her irresponsible. He said that you give when you are fine, and they, he stated, were not fine.

Regina wasn't sure what to do. She wanted to keep stress low in their family but also felt they owed something to their elders. So she asked her husband if they and their two daughters could volunteer at the center. He didn't love the idea, but she pushed and said it was important for the girls.

The next month, they joined other community members on the Saturday volunteer day for the center's art and bake sale. Regina and her daughters brought cookies, while the center provided paper and paints for the girls to draw on. They then sold the pictures at the same table as the beverages and baked goods. The girls loved it. They also made paintings for the seniors at the center and asked their parents if they could go every week.

As you can imagine, Alex changed his mind about the monthly gift. When he saw firsthand how each dollar was put to use to host arts and crafts and exercise programs for the seniors, he said it made a difference to see their money at work in support of senior citizens. He told his wife he wanted to set a good example for their daughters and felt they could make the $50 donation work.

As the months progressed, Regina, Alex, and daughters continued to volunteer. One Saturday, while talking with another volunteer, Alex shared that he was still looking for work. The other volunteer said he might know of something and he'd let him know. The following Saturday, the volunteer approached Alex and asked if he could interview that week at the company where he was employed. One month later, Alex had a job.

Staying connected to your community and giving back during difficult times won't guarantee you employment, but staying holed up inside your house certainly won't have you meeting people and knowing what opportunities are available. Later, Alex asked the other volunteer why he got him the interview, he said that any guy who would give of his time when he was looking for work was someone with the right work ethic for the company.

Rising to Your Generosity Potential

During his presidential acceptance speech, President Barack Obama said of government, "The question we ask today is not whether our government is too big or too small but whether it works." The same approach holds true for giving. The question we ask about giving is not whether we should give or shouldn't, nor how much, but what is required of us.

To most powerfully awaken the change agent within, we must identify and rise to our own generosity potential. We must look closely at those causes we care about most and ask: to allow this vision to thrive, what is my best and most powerful contribution?

While philanthropic advisers, like myself, can offer formulas, percentages, and best practices in giving during lean times, it is up to you to unearth your truest giving potential. No one person can say that you will be most fulfilled and activated if you give *x* amount. Only *you* know what your deepest generosity looks like in action.

To help you in uncovering your generosity potential, I offer you the following three things you can do, starting right now. They will infuse hope and hurrah into your giving and will reconnect you with the joy that comes from giving to your potential:

1. **Define generosity.** What does generosity mean to you? Is your definition different for others than for you? If you don't call yourself a generous person, what actions would you have to take to step into that space? Here are a few ways you can begin to think about what generosity looks like when giving of your time, treasure, and talent:

- Being generous does not mean making a charitable gift that you cannot afford. However, being generous *does* mean writing any size check, even if you're worried about money.

- Being generous does not mean overextending yourself to a point of fatigue and burnout. However, being generous does mean revisiting the priorities you set and ensuring that the material does not supersede the spiritual.
- Being generous does not mean allowing others to take advantage of your talents and gifts. However, being generous does mean offering your talents and gifts without expectation of return.

Generosity is about an amount that is a reach, a stretch for you. While some may see your gift amount as small, if you stretched, you will know your gifts are a reflection of your deepest generosity potential. In the same vein, some may see your name in a newsletter or on a plaque and say, "What a generous person." Only you will know if the gift that generated the accolades was a true measure of your generosity.

2. **Be the change.** No surprise here: Mahatma Gandhi was right when he said, "Be the change you wish to see in the world." We cannot create the possible until we practice and live the improbable. What does that look like in your life? Your community? Do the thing that others keep telling you cannot be done: turn philanthropy on its head by naming yourself a philanthropist even if you aren't wealthy or don't come from an affluent family; learn everything you can about the cause you care about most, and then commit to making this cause a regular and constant force in your life; decide today that you will volunteer two hours a week for the rest of your life, and do not break that commitment.

When you step into the possibility of change, you will worry less about how much to give. You will write your checks to the measure of your vision, commitment, and *chutzpah*, and as a result, you will give to your generosity potential.

3. **Be "irresponsible."** I recently heard a financial expert say, "We have to cut back, even in our charitable giving. If you're facing an uncertain future, it is irresponsible to continue giving at the level you've been giving."

Color me irresponsible! If it is irresponsible to invest in social service, social change, and social justice, then I would like to be counted among the legions of irresponsibles. When you hear advice that is couched in being responsible but it seems to you to stem from anxiety and fear, reconsider the advice. Generosity transforms us because it invites us to give in *all* the ways we can, at *all* the times we can. Generosity asks us to leave Plato's cave and recognize our connectivity and our responsibility toward that connectivity.

Today, be irresponsible. Be bold, powerful, and unapologetic about the checks you write to the causes that are nearest to your heart. You will not regret it, and you will have opened up an expansive world that will ripple through you and out into the world.

7
Position Yourself for Success
Five Keys to an Effective Generosity Plan

As we've explored, values, priorities, and focus make for a successful Generosity Plan. To add even greater depth and impact to your plan, consider what I have discovered to be the five keys to most successful generosity plans: vision, boldness, authenticity, staying the course, and support. Of course to have a highly successful plan, you must—like with the concepts and practice of generosity and charity—know what success looks like to you.

At this book's beginning, you had an opportunity to think about what generosity means to you. You've considered generosity—and philanthropy—in new and more expansive ways. You've likely come to learn that generosity is not defined by writing big checks but by making a habit of giving of yourself in support of that which you care about most. Deep generosity is feeling your integral role in making the world a better place and then acting on that passion every day, in every way you can.

As you become more connected to generosity and know what it means to you, your Generosity Plan will become a living, breathing force in your life. Your plan will be an expression and an extension of your hopes, dreams, and desires for the world. As it deepens its role in your life and your family's life, you will of course want to be certain it is working. You will want to see results. You will want to know your efforts are making a difference. In short, you will want to be successful.

To be sure that you achieve success with your Generosity Plan, let's start by defining it. As with generosity, charity, and money, you can only know if each is working for you if you know how you define them. In the same vein, you've got to know how you define success and its purpose in order to know that you've achieved it.

Defining and measuring success varies, depending on your values. Some people define success as financial, while others define it as familial, material, spiritual, professional, or personal. Some seek achievement or overachievement in every aspect of life. Others seek to live more quietly and to see their successes achieved through their children or grandchildren. Success can be as loaded a word as *money*. When thought of in black and white—I'm either successful or I'm not—success can feel like a pressure cooker. We want to be successful in whatever we do, but how will we know when we get there? What are our personal benchmarks that show us success?

Are you unsuccessful if you didn't get a promotion you wanted? Are you successful if you got a job you didn't think you could get? Are you unsuccessful if you reach a certain age and haven't saved as much money as the financial planning calculators say you should have saved? Are you successful if you have saved more than you need for retirement?

For you to feel fulfilled, nurtured, and fed by your Generosity Plan, you need to think about what will make it a successful plan. You need to answer the question: how do I define success?

And then expand that answer. Explore what success looks like to you. In the past when you've felt successful, why did you feel that way? Was it getting the job or promotion, or was the success in the hours or years you invested to get it?

A few years back, I was giving a keynote address at the Association of Women Business Centers' Annual Conference, and at the end of the speech, during the question-and-answer period, someone from the audience asked me which books on leadership she should read to really become successful. I paused for a minute before I answered her. I wanted to be sure she knew that success and successful people were all around her; they weren't just the good folks who hit the *New York Times* bestseller list. For certain, bestselling authors have achieved success. However, many will tell you that it wasn't hitting a certain number of book sales that made them feel successful. It was sitting down and punching out a huge novel, one character and one word at a time. Success was not quitting when they wanted to quit. Success was not taking themselves too seriously but making time for their kids' favorite cartoon shows even when they had a major deadline to meet.

I told her that if she wanted to learn about leadership, she should look around the room and then look at herself. If she wanted to find success, she should look at her own life and remember times when she wanted to throw in the towel professionally but kept going because her organization's mission statement was too important. She wanted to know what made a successful leader and which books would tell her that. While there are extraordinary books on the market about successful leaders, the secret of success is that you achieve it after you've defined it on your terms and then live up to those terms.

Big names, big causes, big wallets—that's one kind of success, but what does success look like to you?

While *to succeed* is defined as "to come next after another in office or position or in possession of an estate," *success*, in its most encompassing sense, means "to turn out well; to attain a desired object or end."

What will it look like to have your Generosity Plan turn out well? In creating your Generosity Plan, what is your desired end?

Janet

After Janet completed the exercises for her Generosity Plan, she was excited. She had laid out on paper her vision, favorite causes, and how she would wisely use her time, treasure, and talent. Then we discussed success. What, I asked her, will success look like for you?

This was a complicated question for Janet. She laughed and asked if we could go back to the easier discussion about how she felt about money. For Janet, success is a concept layered with a lot of stress. She grew up in a household that strongly emphasized higher education. For Janet's parents, there was nothing more important than the need for Janet and her siblings to attend and finish college. While her parents would do whatever they could to make this happen—help with studying, save money for school, get the books and supplies they'd need to excel—they expected Janet and her siblings to "buckle down." This meant they were expected to always do their homework, master each subject, and not "horse around" when they should be studying.

Study they did. They worked hard. They quizzed each other. They got the grades they needed to get. All five children went on to colleges where they all did well in their fields of study. All five graduated with honors.

After college, Janet went on to get her graduate and doctorate degrees and to teach biology at a four-year institution. She loved her work and the students; Janet was a student of learning. If she was going to take on an endeavor, she was going to go full force—and she was going to succeed.

When it came to our conversation about success, Janet felt anxious. She wasn't sure how to define success for her favorite causes. She told me it's not like preparing for an exam when you can just read the chapters, do the work, prepare, sleep well, eat well, and likely get a good grade. She said that it made her feel frustrated that no matter how hard she worked on her Generosity Plan, her favorite cause may still not have the desired end, after all her hard work. In fact, during the course of talking about success for her Generosity Plan and her favorite causes, Janet thought maybe she shouldn't continue. She couldn't see how to gauge success and felt that without being able to measure it, this plan may be an exercise in futility.

I was thrilled when we came to this moment because it is at the moment of feeling hopeless that we need our Generosity Plan the most; at that moment, our Generosity Plan fully forms itself. Janet felt great about the concrete steps throughout the plan—*a* plus *b* equals *c*. She was even okay to stretch a bit, provided there was a concrete and tangible outcome at the end. How, she wondered, could she consider her plan or her efforts a success if the cause she cared about most—conservation—would not be "fixed" during her lifetime?

For Janet, success means achievement. She defines *success* as "getting the results you want as a result of doing what is required of you." She isn't wrong. Success can certainly be results and outcomes. But what, I asked Janet, is your desired end for you in creating this Generosity Plan? What value will be brought to your life as a result of living a generous and giving life?

As Janet explored this, she shared that she decided to create this plan to be as good to the world as it had been to her. She wanted to give back because she had been given so much. She said that as she stepped up the professional ladder, she often found herself immersed in competition and outdoing others. Janet also said she felt she had stopped being a generous person and thought that if generosity, giving, and kindness came into the picture, someone would succeed her and she would be left out. This feeling worried her. She shared that when she first heard about the Generosity

Plan, she thought about the word *generosity* all day. She wondered when she had last been as generous to anyone as her parents had been to her and her siblings.

I asked her if success is only achieving a goal, or could it be that success is also the working toward her cause's goals and living her life in service to those goals? Could there be success in living a generous life?

Janet wasn't completely sold. She wanted to like this notion, but her type A personality had her focused on results and outcomes.

I shared with her the story of Michael.

Michael

I met Michael only once, at a fundraising event. I learned from him that his cause and passion was juvenile diabetes. We talked for a while, and he told me his story. Later, friends shared with me other pieces that helped me create a more complete picture of how Michael's definition of success actually led him to leave his passion.

For years, Michael worked tirelessly for juvenile diabetes; he went full force. He was a terrific fundraiser and a powerful advocate. He talked about the cause whenever he could to whomever would listen. Then, as the years progressed, Michael's enthusiasm waned. He was frustrated that there hadn't been a cure. While he applauded the work in caring for young people with diabetes and assisting families as they helped their children manage the illness, he wanted a cure. He felt his efforts, though helpful, did not produce his desired outcome. Because there hasn't yet been a cure for juvenile diabetes, Michael felt that he and others in the cause hadn't succeeded. He eventually left the cause altogether.

Michael couldn't see the success in the trying, the coming together, the making the invisible visible, the families no longer being alone or without adequate information, the families who couldn't afford insulin but received it through philanthropic efforts. To him, success meant a cure. To him, success did not mean each of us doing what we can, with what we have, where we are. In Michael's eyes, the best of our abilities was not good enough.

Maybe Michael had a point: until we accomplish our cause's end goal, we haven't had success. However, if that were true, if the goal were the end game, why was Michael no longer in the game? If going forward with tunnel vision and pushing and pushing for one big goal were the solution, wouldn't we have had the cure to countless diseases and social ills already?

What if the best of Michael's time, treasure, and talents was yet to come? What if Michael speaking at one more event would be just the spark needed for someone else to get involved and give all they have to the cause? And what if that person held a key to meeting the goal?

What is certain is that without Michael, juvenile diabetes has one less advocate—one less champion giving his time, treasure, and talent.

What if Michael had instead expanded his definition of success? What if he had seen success as caring for those who were struggling with the illness while working toward a cure? Or ensuring that low-income families had the tools and supplies needed while working toward a cure? What role could generosity and charity have played in expanding Michael's definition of success?

After much soul-searching, Janet defined success for her Generosity Plan. She wrote, *that I will have the courage to stay true to my vision and cause.* For success for this cause, "That the conservation movement will raise awareness for one person one day at a time until each of us deeply believes in the best for the Earth."

As Janet worked her Generosity Plan based on these definitions of success, she told me that she hadn't faced the burnout she did in her academic career. Instead, she saw victories in small actions and she held herself accountable, seeing success as keeping her word to be courageous for her cause.

What about for you?

Take time to answer in your Generosity Journal:

- How do I define success?
- In the past, what have I done that I considered to be successful? Graduating high school? College? Getting married? Having children? Landing my dream job? Running a marathon? Taking a class I was scared to take?
- Why did I feel successful? Was it in meeting the end goal? Keeping my commitment? Working hard? What defined success for me?

Now, think about your Generosity Plan and think expansively about success. How will you measure your success along the way? What will success look like to you in the next several years?

For Lisa, success in her Generosity Planning is keeping the financial goals she set. Sticking to her 10 percent giving budget for a year is a measure of huge success. This showed she had made and kept a commitment even though she knew it will be tough to juggle.

For Joshua, success in his Generosity Plan is getting his company involved with building housing for low-income families. While Joshua would have liked to see every family in a home and his plan helped him work toward that goal, success to him is getting more of the private sector involved in this effort. That is his contribution to success.

For Leanne, success is never losing sight of her vision while being as bold and strong-willed as she can be every day. As an advocate for women who had faced physical violence in their homes—and as a survivor herself—Leanne sees her success in staying steadfast for the cause and learning to lean on others for support and help. She says that success was the day she left her household of violence, and everything since then is just opening the same door for others.

Janet, Lisa, Joshua, and Leanne opened up for me the real keys to a successful Generosity Plan. They unlocked these secrets by asking themselves the core questions: why am I doing this, and what will it take to make it really work? The *why* for each of them was varied, based on their ideas about generosity, charity, and giving back. The *what will it take?* was all the same: me.

Here, then, are the five keys to a truly successful Generosity Plan and generosity planning experience:

Vision

In chapter 2, you created your vision statement—the hope that would guide the content of your Generosity Plan. You examined the role of vision in choosing charities wisely and giving your time, treasure, and talent to the causes dearest to you. When you unlocked your vision, you began your journey in creating just the right Generosity Plan for you.

As you give your time, treasure, and talent to your favorite causes, you will feel many victories. There will be success stories, triumphs achieved, and hurdles overcome. You will read stories of the difference being made. You will see your contributions in action.

At the same time, there will be difficult moments. You might have worked tirelessly on a local ballot initiative, only to have your initiative defeated. Or you may have given funds to help survivors of a natural disaster, only to hear that just a small percentage of people could be helped while many others continued to suffer. During these moments—and there *will* be these moments—you will need to lean on your vision, your hope for the future, to keep you strong and maintain your momentum.

Feeling down and discouraged is part of the process of making change; staying there isn't. Berkeley Rice said, "Visionary people are visionary partly because of the very great many things they don't see." If you can envision a better world, work your Generosity Plan to make that world possible. Remember why you came to the cause, why it means so much to you, what you hope for, what you hope for those who will come after you. When history looks back, what will it say of us? Will it say you played it safe or that you, despite all odds, gave generously with hope and vision on your side?

When you feel tough times within your cause or your Generosity Plan, how can your vision lift you up and keep you strong and moving forward?

Boldness

People always say that I didn't give up my seat because I was tired, but that isn't true. I was not tired physically, or no more tired than I usually was at the end of a working day. I was not old, although some people have an image of me as being old then. I was forty-two. No, the only tired I was, was tired of giving in.

—ROSA PARKS

On December 1, 1955, during the days of racial segregation in Tuskegee, Alabama, African-American seamstress Rosa Parks took a bold stand by refusing to relinquish her seat on the city bus to a white man. I've often wondered if her heart was beating quickly in her throat or if she was ready for that moment.

Rosa Parks's boldness galvanized the Civil Rights Movement, ushering in a new era of passion, politics, and power. Could she have known by taking that seat that she would come to be known as the mother of the Civil Rights Movement? She held that seat on December 1, 1955, because she was "tired of giving in."

While your Generosity Plan may not involve launching the next phase of a human rights movement—but if it does, work it!—it's very likely that your cause requires boldness. Earlier in the book, we talked about standing in your cause. You looked at what it meant for you to take a stand, and how your unique traits and talents could help you stand in your cause and express your voice.

What does boldness look like to you? How do you imagine that a bold action could benefit your cause?

When Jacki spoke to a group of women business leaders, she said that she felt it was a little too hot in the crowded room. She took off her scarf and jacket to reveal a brilliantly bold Wonder Woman T-shirt. She got up on her chair and flexed her muscles. On that day, and now ever since, Jacki stands for women.

When Marla entered the breast cancer walk, she was terrified. She was worried she would have to rest a lot and was concerned she wouldn't finish; she didn't want to let anyone down. With her friend's support and the thousands of people cheering her on, she boldly entered and finished the walk. To this day, Marla says that being bold helped her discover new parts of her and made her a fierce advocate for breast cancer prevention and research.

Boldness asks you to come out of your comfort zone, if only for a moment. How do you know if you are stepping into boldness? You know you are being your best bold self when you feel excited, nervous, and hopeful in the same moment. You know you are being your best bold self when the action you are about to take will change you inside. Again, bold doesn't have to be big and flashy, but it should be daring for you.

When you are bold for you and your own life, you can feel the change. When you are bold for something bigger than you, you make change. When you are bold with your Generosity Plan, you give a voice to the issues you care about most and you reveal what you are made of. When you think beyond perceived limitations—*I couldn't possibly do that*—you unleash the best of you. Today is the day to think about what a bold act from you will look like to benefit your cause.

The German poet, novelist, and playwright Johann Wolfgang Von Goethe said, "Boldness has genius, power, and magic in it. Begin it now." The moment you do, your cause will be the better for it.

Authenticity

A few years back, *U.S. News & World Report* featured an article titled "Truly Authentic Leadership," by Bill George. In it, George defined authentic leadership and authentic leaders this way:

> *Authentic leaders know the "true north" of their moral compass and are prepared to stay the course despite challenges and disappointments. They are more concerned about serving others than they are about their own success or recognition. Which is not to say that authentic leaders are perfect. Every leader has weaknesses, and all are subject to human frailties and mistakes. Yet by acknowledging failings and admitting error, they connect with people and empower them to take risks.*
>
> *How do we recognize authentic leaders? Usually, they demonstrate these five traits:*
>
> *1. Pursuing their purpose with passion*

2. *Practicing solid values*

3. *Leading with their hearts as well as their heads*

4. *Establishing connected relationships*

5. *Demonstrating self-discipline*[21]

Why include an excerpt on authentic *leadership* in a book about generosity? What does one have to do with the other?

About authentic leadership, George speaks to purpose, passion, values, leading with the heart, connections, relationships, and empowering others for that which is greater than the individual. All of these are true as well for living a generous and charitable life. Authenticity requires us to stay true to our values, vision, strategies, and tactics. It does not ask us to be inflexible or unbending as we learn more from others and grow; it does not ask us to be stubborn and unmovable. But it *does* ask us to be "not false ... true to [our] own personality, spirit, or character."[22]

Authenticity can be admitting when you were wrong about the next best step for your cause and asking others to continue to guide you in your learning. Authenticity can mean putting ego aside and letting someone else get the credit because it benefits your cause even if it doesn't benefit you. Authenticity can mean standing in your own cause even when others tell you it is foolhardy or a waste of time. They might snicker at you and call you naive, but in your heart, you will know that you are being true to your own spirit and hope for the future.

Authenticity is extraordinary because it sometimes seems that it is difficult to come by. As I write this chapter, the United States is in the midst of a recession. We listen to stories of Wall Street business leaders while some politicians tell us things that don't quite strike us as authentic. We hear a certain spin about how the mortgage industry got to such a point of desperation. There seems to be a lot of passing the buck. Mostly, we wonder if someone will just step up and be authentic. "Here's what happened," they could say, "we didn't do what we were supposed to do and we didn't stop it when we could have. Somewhere along the way we had good motivations—a home for every American and a profit for us—but somewhere along the way we ended up on that road that's paved with the best intentions."

Wouldn't that be something? Wouldn't it be transformative to witness leadership being accountable for their mistakes and being true to their character? It may be, though, that our business and political leaders need *you* to model authenticity, not the other way around. The American poet June Jordan said it better than I ever could, "And who will join this standing up?... We are the ones we have been waiting for."

Authenticity is both a tool and a responsibility. Each time you are true to your character and spirit, you make a decision to be authentic. Authenticity can help ensure you spend your time, talents, and treasure where you want to spend them. Authenticity also asks you to do so.

How can authenticity support the goals in your Generosity Plan? What role can being true to your own spirit and character play as you move forward with your charitable work?

About living a life that reflects your spirit and your truth, Mother Teresa said, "Honesty and transparency make you vulnerable. Be honest and transparent anyway."

Staying the Course

Of the five keys to the Generosity Plan, staying the course is my personal favorite. Not because Wikipedia defines it as "a phrase used in the context of a war or battle meaning to pursue a goal regardless of any obstacles or criticism." That's not my definition.

For those of us who have been involved in social service and social change work for decades, staying the course means being there for the long haul and not getting distracted by the cause of the month.

I know you know what I mean by *cause of the month*. We see it most often with celebrities or big fundraising galas. Whereas one month prostate cancer is the hot topic, the next month, it's colon cancer. While these media blitzes can be good for the cause, the real work happens day in and day out. The real change happens over the long haul. The difference is made when we stay the course with our cause versus getting involved in everything that becomes visible or high profile.

Staying the course let's you know that your vision is sound, your boldness intact, and your authenticity front and center. Staying the course means that you will be there for your cause through the good times and bad, successes and drawbacks, wins and losses, and ups and downs. Staying the course means you truly believe in what you say you believe and you will stand in this effort for as long as it takes.

Staying the course doesn't mean ignoring new interests that come up or neglecting an urgent need. You might give your time, treasure, and talents to preserving national parks, and you may have been involved in this effort for a long while. It is your heart-and-soul work, and you will be involved and support it for as long as you live. At the same time, when you learn about a family who lost their home to a fire, you may give a donation to the local Red Cross or to a shelter. By giving to urgent needs, you aren't abandoning your cause. It is still your priority. You are just helping to meet an emerging need.

Staying the course—not getting pulled from cause to cause to cause—can be difficult. With the ever-increasing challenges of our world, it can be easy to sway from one cause to another. The media bring to our computers and televisions the new issue, country, disease, epidemic that demands immediate attention. Wanting to do the right thing, we sometimes leave the issue we have been working on to run to one that has recently became spotlighted for us.

While we should not ignore an urgent or emerging need, we also should not abandon our core vision work. If the emerging need expands our vision and we want to include it in the heart of our Generosity Plan, then we should do so. What's most important is not which causes or efforts you get involved with but that you spend the time to get to know them, stay through the good and bad, and become one of the champions of the cause.

When you stay for the long haul, you will love what you learn. You will see changes you didn't think could happen in your lifetime, and you will become one of the experts. You'll even get to say "back in the day" about your cause to educate the next round of people who are stepping in and stepping up.

I got involved in protecting the lives of animals when I was a wee one. I remember being twelve or thirteen years old and knocking on the doors of my neighbors. Did you know, I asked, that a factory farm is moving into our town and they are grinding up baby male chicks while they're still alive? I was a very popular kid in my neighborhood.

Since that day, I have supported animals in any way I can. Caring for animals and helping ease their suffering is a core part of my vision and my own Generosity Plan. There have been some very tough moments over the years. During these times, I have leaned on vision to keep me moving forward and going strong; I have taken bold steps, none of which I regret taking; and I have stayed authentic about my passion for animal welfare even when others thought my thinking was a little crazy. I've also stayed the course. And, in the twenty-five years of working for animal well-being, I have been honored to witness remarkable changes in the world. While there is much more work to be done, I have seen shifts in attitude, changes in legislation, and the passing of new national and international law. Where once the food choices for vegetarians at restaurants was water and an iceberg lettuce salad, today almost every restaurant you go into has a vegetarian item or will be happy to accommodate your request.

I'm so glad I've stayed the course. While the road has had its share of potholes, I know that my staying the course is good for the cause, good for my own giving, and instrumental in making change.

Staying the course is longevity, and longevity makes real, lasting advancements. Hang in there with your cause. You will be very glad you did.

Support

The fifth key to a successful Generosity Plan is support. We all need support. Being held up and cheered on by our loved ones can make a difference between "I can't do it" and "Watch me go!"

Because support has a range of meanings and applications, it can show up in a variety of ways. *Support* means to "keep from weakening or failing; provide for or maintain; hold in position; bear the weight of; and aid the cause."

Here are the types of support Natalie, Bob, and Amelia asked for to ensure that they moved forward full force with their Generosity Plans.

Natalie: "Keep me from feeling low when change takes time!"

An outdoor enthusiast, Natalie was committed to clean air and clean water. As a kid growing up in the Midwest, Natalie remembered her dad taking her to swim and fish in the summer, hike in the fall, play ice hockey in the winter, and trail walk in the spring. Though Natalie and her family didn't have a lot of money, she felt privileged to be able to experience nature. As an adult, Natalie worked as a park ranger and was passionate about keeping America's parks healthy and strong. She had also extended her passion to clean water globally.

Throughout the years, Natalie had gotten heavily involved in efforts to keep rivers and lakes clean and to reduce carbon emissions. As this work was not free from stress and setbacks, Natalie found herself feeling frustrated and defeated. She loved reading the success stories, and when she did, she felt hopeful about progress being made. She didn't do as well when she read statistics about the lack of clean drinking water for people throughout the world, low-quality air in major cities, and the erosion and disappearance of open land and wetlands.

As a result over the years, Natalie weaved in and out of involvement in clean air and clean water campaigns. While she told herself that her weaving was a reflection of her life getting busier at key intervals, the truth was she made her life a bit busier during her cause's tough times so she could avoid the eventual overwhelm and hopelessness. Eventually, after a cooling off period, she would find herself ready to go again, only to repeat the cycle of ducking in and out after reengaging for a while.

For Natalie to fully live her Generosity Plan, to move forward powerfully on her vision of creating a healthier, cleaner world, she recognized she needed some kind of support, but she couldn't identify what could be available to her that would make a difference.

As she explored support, she resonated most with needing it to "keep from weakening or failing." She then shared with her friends her tendency to go in and out of activism mode and that she wanted to change so she could really stand in the cause consistently. She said she would take mini-breaks (as we all should!), with the emphasis on breaks versus full-on sabbaticals.

She told her friends that her problem was that she felt defeated and beaten up by the seeming lack of progress in creating a healthier world. She asked if they could help her prevent burnout.

Her friends heard her and agreed to help. They set in motion a plan to keep Natalie connected, inspired, and proud of the achievements that were being made. Every week, her friends would email or MySpace a success story regarding clean water and fresh air. They'd send her shout-outs for the work she was doing and tell her not to give up, that successes can be found every day. For her birthday, Natalie's friends pooled their money and bought carbon offsets in Natalie's name. They reminded her that the work she was doing now—though sometimes tough—was for the next generation and that, for it, we all need to stay focused and strong.

Natalie's friends felt invigorated by giving her support, and two of them made the environment their number-one cause. And Natalie got exactly what she needed: the support to stay the course and accept tough times as temporary setbacks that merely tested her resolve to make a real, lasting difference.

Today, Natalie doesn't focus on the negative. She knows that she can't do it all, and she avoids reading those stories that keep her from staying active and connected. As a result, she has stepped up her efforts on the environment and has added a "Success" section to her Generosity Journal for those days when she needs an extra dose of inspiration.

In addition, she also reminds herself that to keep from weakening or failing, she needed to go back to doing the outdoor activities she used to do with her dad. While her work had her outdoors all day, she realized she was so busy protecting nature she wasn't spending time enjoying nature. She found that she could draw strength and support from the very thing she worked to care for, so she decided to add rock climbing to her life. Now when she is working on campaigns for clean water and air—which usually have her on her computer—she remembers the feeling of rock climbing. This feeling inspires her to go that extra step. She remembers the tough parts of the rock and somehow finding it in her to hoist herself closer to the top. She leans on these skills to get her over the difficult obstacles in making social change.

Lastly, she realizes that what she does today matters. She knows that the next generation will get to enjoy the outdoors as she has, in part because she is doing what she can, staying the course, getting support, and leaving behind her practice of weaving in and out.

Bob: "Even if it's not your top cause, support my cause once a year in any way you can!"

Alec, Bob's son, was diagnosed with autism when he was two years old. Like many parents, Bob was angry, scared, and uncertain about what to do. A person of action, Bob quickly took to learning everything he could about the disease, including the newest research and treatments, therapies, and family support. Seemingly overnight, he became a champion for the cause, for his son, and for other families like his own.

Because of the stress that can be associated with raising a child with autism, many friends thought the kind of support Bob would need was a listening ear or a shoulder. But Bob managed his stress through running and cycling, and used the rest of his free time to raise awareness about and fundraise for autism research. Because they weren't providing emotional support, Bob's friends weren't sure how to help.

The support that Bob asked for was aid to the cause. He asked his friends, distant relatives, coworkers, dry cleaner, dentist, anyone in his immediate circle to do one thing a year for autism awareness. When he was hosting a fundraiser, he asked his dry cleaner if he would hang a flyer in his store window. When he had news to share about a breakthrough therapy, he asked his friends to circulate it to their online mailing list. When his birthday came around, he asked his coworkers if they could forego a cake and instead send the pooled money to his favorite autism nonprofit.

For Bob, support means having encouraging people show up for the cause. He doesn't want friends and colleagues to feel they had to make autism their number-one priority, but he did ask if once a year they could make a small gesture or act. He emphasized that awareness and education among networks was often more valuable than a check.

Bob's extended circle is happy to help. One person spreads the word about autism on his blog. Another friend posts information about upcoming fundraisers on her LinkedIn page. A colleague who works at a law firm shares the information with her fellow attorneys, some of whom ended up getting more involved in the cause.

Bob is a fearless and tireless advocate for autism research and a cure. As one of his Generosity Plan goals is to "make as much noise as I can to increase funding, and to ensure care for families," support meant getting more people involved to meet his vision of "a world of healthy children."

Amelia: "Help me get to giving away 5 percent!"

In the world of people who spend money and people who save money, Amelia is a spender. She makes a modest salary and had few debts, but she enjoys spending money on dinner and drinks, CDs, DVDs, jewelry, and clothes. Shopping is a fun outlet for her, offering time with friends while treating her to new things. She has always felt a little remorseful about her spending but not so much that she wants to cut back drastically.

However, this feeling changed when her friend, who had suffered from depression throughout their friendship, overdosed on prescription medication and died. Amelia was shattered. For months she was withdrawn, guilt-ridden, and devastated. As she worked through her grief and began to feel stronger in herself, she felt she wanted to do something but wasn't sure what that could be. And she didn't want to just do something one time; she wanted to learn more about mental illness, its warning signs, and therapies available to people who were suffering and to their loved ones. She didn't want others to be as devastated as she had felt and as alone as she imagined her friend had felt.

After creating her Generosity Plan, Amelia realized that she would be more fulfilled if she spent a little less on things for herself and put some of this money into the charities she learned about which were helping people with mental health issues, as well as their friends and families. She started by giving $20 here and $25 there, but this didn't feel like enough. She felt disconnected—like she was giving in response to requests versus being active in her giving. She decided to create a giving budget and agreed that she would give 3 percent of her earnings to an organization that helped youth who were at-risk for depression and suicide. But before she could begin giving her time and get deeply involved, she knew she needed to take the time to deal with the emotional impact of her friend's overdose.

After grieving and getting support, Amelia ultimately decided that her commitment to her cause would be to cut back on personal spending and begin to give away 5 percent of her income. This was a stretch for her. She found herself slipping back into spending when she felt the grief associated with her friend's loss.

So she talked to her parents and friends and told them what she wanted to do. Everyone encouraged her to try to reach the 5 percent as one of the tools to manage her grief and a powerful way to honor her friend's memory. Her mother suggested she figure out what her 5 percent would total and then make a plan to fundraise that same amount from friends and relatives. She loved this idea of being able to double her contribution to the youth organization.

Amelia needed the support of friends and family to help her create a larger goal for her giving. When she realized she would be asking them for money to match her giving amount, she felt a new sense of accountability for her own giving. If people she cared about were going to write a check to this charity knowing that Amelia would be doing the same, she would have to keep that commitment.

Of course, to be an effective fundraiser, Amelia had to get to know more about the organization. Even though she didn't yet want to work as a volunteer with young people, she did want to learn more about the work being done. She visited the organization and learned about the support groups, early intervention programs, and outreach and education efforts. She asked great questions about what really works to help young people who are at risk. While she was sad that her friend did not know about this resource when he was suffering, she felt his death would not be in vain if she could be a part of helping another young person who may be suffering.

Throughout her fundraising efforts, Amelia began to heal from her friend's death. She saw firsthand the impact of the good work of the organization, and felt proud of herself for cutting back on spending so she could support a cause that had become dear to her.

For Amelia, support was not having to go it alone. Support was asking for guidance on how to meet her 5 percent goal. Because she elicited the support of people who cared about her healing and who were in support of her helping young people suffering with depression and anxiety, she was able to hit her first goal of 5 percent and double her giving through her matching fundraising program.

About this experience, Amelia said that she thought her friend would be proud of her. He was a warm and sensitive person who always helped others when he could. She felt she had stepped up for him and his memory, and she didn't miss the new purse she would have bought.

What type of support do you need to reach your goals? How could enlisting support help you be more accountable and more successful? If your friends or family could do one thing for you that would make a difference in meeting your Generosity Plan goals, what would it be?

Getting support is the difference between lasting a little while and lasting for the long haul. Getting support is the difference between doing something once or twice and making that something an integral part of your life. It is okay to need help, and it is okay to ask for help; social change does not happen in a vacuum or single-handedly. Doing the work together brings better results and makes for success today and tomorrow.

8
Maintaining Momentum
Managing Naysayers and Distractions

*I*n the United States, New Year's Day (January 1st), is also known as Resolution Day. It is the day many resolve to lose weight, exercise more, read more, watch less television, run a mile every day, spend less time at work, spend more time at home, learn a language. You name it. With sheer will, we sign up for the gym, buy foods with whole wheat in the ingredients list, and leave work at 5 PM.

That is, until February 1. All of a sudden, we're a bit less enthusiastic than we were a month before. We've lost some steam, and we're not making the headway we thought we would. Work pressures mount, and we're staying at the office until 6 or 7 PM. We hit snooze instead of hitting the gym, and white pasta starts looking good again.

Why don't we keep our resolutions? Do we lack the will? The resolve? Do we really not want to achieve the goals we set? Turns out we don't lack the will or the resolve. We do in fact want to reach our physical, financial, and emotional goals. What trips us up in keeping to our goals are:

- Going too fast out of the gate
- Not having a plan to maintain momentum
- Getting stopped in our tracks by naysayers and distractions

These are true for your Generosity Plan as well. We are excited to get behind a cause, and we dive right in. I know a woman who sold four hundred boxes of Girl Scout Cookies for her daughter in one week. Four hundred boxes. By the time week two came, she couldn't stand the word *Tagalongs* any longer. She was already exhausted and couldn't see how she could keep up at the pace she set. Within seven days, she lost her momentum and, with it, her enthusiasm. She never sold box number four hundred and one.

Though Girl Scout Cookie selling season is short–lived (and we can get overwhelmed even during short-lived projects), creating a better world takes time, healthy momentum, and the capacity to navigate the distractions and the naysayers. What then are the secrets of those people who stay engaged, involved, and invigorated year after year? The solution is in knowing what we need to learn when we engage in a new endeavor and by asking for support when we meet roadblocks along the way.

Earlier in the book, we talked about one of the hurdles you would face on your journey: not seeing progress for your cause. We looked at ways to stay connected to the small victories to keep you inspired even during the tough times. We talked about seeking support, celebrating the victories, and knowing that setbacks are as much a part of the process as the successes.

Now we're going to take the next step and examine what it takes to keep momentum when you are faced with naysayers and distractions. We will look at and name these momentum squashers—and there are plenty—and create an antidote for each.

The top two momentum squashers are naysayers, those well-meaning folks who want to help you get your head out of the clouds and see the world for what it is, and personal distractions, those obstacles we erect that get in our own way. I'm a particular expert on personal distractions and will be happy to share with you how I have gotten in my own way many, many times, and the tools

I've used that resulted in less time wasted and more time making amazing change happen.

Momentum Squasher #1: Naysayers

Imagine you are feeling great about your Generosity Plan. You are reading this book. You have created a Generosity Journal. You are looking back to your giving roots, naming your vision, and clarifying your priorities. You have looked at how you can give your time, treasure, and talent to help your cause. You have thoughtfully considered how you can take a stand, and how you can express your voice to make a positive difference. You have examined your ideas about generosity, charity, money, and giving back. You have opened up your heart to the change agent within and feel a strong light inside of you. You know you can and will make a difference. You know that you are the one you have always been waiting for.

Then, you meet a naysayer.

"I'm not sure why you're going to all this effort. You're just one person. Even if you help a little, nothing is going to change."

"Animal rights? Are you kidding? Children are starving and going without the basics. There are wars and genocide everywhere, and you're trying to protect a pig?"

"It's nice, but don't you think you should leave this to the experts? I mean, there are people with PhDs who can't figure out how to end poverty or cure diseases. Do you really think you're going to have an impact?"

I'm guessing you might have met one of these people before. I think it's possible I've met them all. And at first, I felt shut down by their words. I was angry that they'd burst my balloon, hurt that they could take something that mattered so much to me and dismiss it in a sentence. I was plagued with self-doubt: *Maybe they're right. Maybe I won't be able to help. Maybe what I'm doing could be undone in one minute by the signing of a bill or the transfer of money from one big bank to another. Maybe my efforts are too small to really matter.*

As you step up into your Generosity Plan, you will meet these naysayers. You may even have a naysayer voice in you. Here is what I have learned that I hope can be helpful to you: if people are living the life they want to live and doing what they think is right, they will not be upset or threatened by you living the life you want and doing what you think is right.

Think about the last time someone told you about something new they were embarking on. Perhaps your friend decided to go back to school. Maybe someone you know wanted to open her own business. Or maybe your spouse wanted to take up running after a lifetime of being sedentary. How did you respond? If you were happy for them and offered your support, chances are, their leap wasn't something you've always wanted but haven't felt courage enough to do. If, however, you found yourself questioning them ("Are you sure now's the right time in this economy?" or "A marathon? Isn't that a pretty big goal for someone who doesn't even walk to the mailbox?"), chances are, their going for big goals is holding up a mirror to you. Chances are, there is a big goal you want, but the naysayer within has kept you from going after it. Chances are, you don't necessarily doubt their capacity to make a goal a reality (unless they have tried dozens of times and have not made headway), but what you are really feeling is, *Why haven't I gone after my big goal?*

If you have ever known this feeling, then you can identify with the naysayers you will meet when it comes to living your Generosity Plan. Their crankiness isn't about you; it's about them. This is good news. It means you don't have to defend or explain yourself. You don't have to make the case for why you are choosing this charity or why you are going to New Orleans to help build housing in the Lower Ninth Ward. You don't have to engage in debate, point out why they are mistaken, or get them to understand your point of view.

Instead, you have a few options: say nothing, nod and smile, or use any of the responses below that I have used on more than one occasion.

- *"I'm not sure why you're going to all this effort. You're just one person. Even if you help a little nothing is going to change."* You know, I used to feel the exact same way. Then I created a Generosity Plan, started reading about other people like me making a difference, and realized that if I don't do my part, I'm the weak link in the chain. Alone, I can't do it, but without me, it can't get done.
- *"Your priority area is the environment? How can you be thinking about trees when people don't even have jobs? I suppose now you want to take away jobs from people in the lumber industry?"* Before I got more involved, I thought it could only be one or the other. I really did think the environment and jobs were pitted against each other. I've learned differently, but it sounds like you think they *are* against one another. Can you tell me more about that?
- *"Animal rights? Are you kidding? Children are starving and going without the basics. There are wars and genocide everywhere and you're trying to protect a pig?"* That's a good point. Can you tell me what you're involved in around helping starving children? I'd love to know more about that.
- *"Good luck with what you're doing, but there are people controlling the strings and they are corrupt. It doesn't matter if you make headway, they'll find a way to pull the rug out from under you just when you think you're getting ahead."* I know, and it's wrong. What do you think we should do about it?
- *"In the end, no one is watching out for you but you. You gotta take care of number one first 'cause while you're busy being a do-gooder, no one's going to be doing anything for you."* I

haven't had that experience. Did someone tell you that would happen, or have you experienced it firsthand?

- *"It's nice, but don't you think you should leave this to the experts? I mean, there are people with PhDs who can't figure out how to end poverty or cure diseases. Do you really think you're going to have an impact?"* Yes.

When you meet a naysayer, hold up those Wonder Woman deflector bracelets and just send the negative thoughts back. You may never change their minds and they may always think you're naive, but that's okay. Maintaining momentum isn't about changing other people's thinking. It's about maintaining your own.

What's tough about naysaying is that sometimes the negative banter doesn't come from without, but it sources from within. Sometimes you may find yourself wondering, *What am I doing? Why am I doing it? Is it really helping? Maybe I should go to a department store and spend every last generosity dime on me.* This is part of the process. If it was always easy, you wouldn't deepen your commitment to the cause. You are supposed to question. You are supposed to feel down. You are supposed to feel uncertain. You maintain momentum when you let the space for those thoughts emerge, give them a little room, then boot them to side, knowing that they are not serving your generosity goals. If they stick around for even longer, ask a friend to help you get past the negative thinking. When you do, and you meet the naysayer within, or a naysayer at work or in your family, you will have dealt with the demons. It will be easier from there.

More Tips to Keep You Strong

Sometimes the people you hope will give you support will not. Either they disagree with your area of interest or they are frustrated with themselves for not taking action. When you begin taking action for your passion, you could be met with resistance. While rejection of your Generosity Plan can feel defeating or even maddening, you never know the impact your actions can have, especially on those who resist your efforts the most.

Don't apologize for what you care about. You are following your heart and your passion. This requires no apologies or explanations. When we face rejection or criticism, we often defend ourselves: "Well, of course I care about children in the United States. In fact, one of the groups I give to funds doctors visiting children who live far away from hospitals." It is a tempting response, to be sure, but not necessary. Instead, you can reply in a few other ways: "I appreciate your thoughts. My passion, though, is on the international arena," or "I don't know too much about work being done in the United States for children. Can you tell me what you're involved in?"

Choose people who will support you based upon what support looks like to you. Earlier in the book, you might have jotted down your responses to "The support I need from friends and family...." For my friend Lisa, support is accountability. For others, support is listening, sharing interest in learning about your Generosity Plan, accompanying you to events or volunteer opportunities, or chopping vegetables for the house party you are hosting for a nonprofit organization. Determine the support you need. Be clear about it. Then approach the people who want you to be successful in pursuing your passions. Ask them for specific support. Involve them in your Generosity Plan.

And for those who question why you are getting involved in living a deeply generous life, you can share with them that generosity, it seems, does more than just make the world a better place; it improves your health and makes you rich.

The mission of privately held and funded nonprofit Random Acts of Kindness Foundation is to "inspire people to practice kindness and pass it on to others." As part of its education and outreach about the power of kindness, on September 11, 2008, the foundation released an article titled "Kindness: How Good Deeds Can Be Good for You." The article outlines the health benefits of giving back, primarily drawing from the work of Allan Luks, who served as the executive director of Big Brothers Big Sisters of New York City for eighteen years. Now in his mid-sixties, Luks is a passionate advocate for getting individuals involved in volunteerism, believing firmly in the "helper's high."

"Kindness: How Good Deeds Can Be Good For You"

In the late 1980s and early 1990s, former executive director of Big Brothers/Big Sisters of New York City, Allan Luks, surveyed U.S. volunteers in an effort to learn about possible health benefits associated with giving back.

Luks' study involved more than 3,000 volunteers of all ages at more than 20 organizations throughout the country. He sent a 17-question survey to these volunteers, asking them how they felt when they did a kind act. A total of 3,296 surveys were returned to Luks, and after a computerized analysis, he saw a clear cause-and-effect relationship between helping and good health. In a nutshell, Luks' concluded, "Helping contributes to the maintenance of good health, and it can diminish the effect of diseases and disorders both serious and minor, psychological and physical."

The volunteers in Luks' study testified to feeling a rush of euphoria, followed by a longer period of calm, after performing a kind act. This feeling, which Luks calls "helper's high," involves physical sensations that strongly indicate a sharp reduction in stress and the release of the body's natural painkillers, the endorphins. This initial rush is then followed by a longer-lasting period of improved emotional well-being.[23]

And, as if improving your physical and emotional health isn't a powerful enough motivator to move forward with your Generosity Plan, for those of you more inclined to the economics of generosity, research is beginning to reveal that giving money to charity actually makes you rich. Is this possible? How can taking money out of my bank account increase my financial worth?

In his November 2008 article, "Giving Makes You Rich: New Proof that It Pays to Be Charitable," author and professor Arthur C. Brooks shares how giving stimulates personal earnings and increases financial prosperity for a nation.

> *The Social Capital Community Benchmark Survey, completed in 2000, is a survey of about 30,000 people in more than 40 communities across the U.S. and is the best single source of data available on the civic participation of Americans. The S.C.C.B.S., which takes into account differences in education, age, race, religion, and other personal characteristics, shows that people who give charitably make significantly more money than those who don't. While that seems like common sense, it turns out that the link in the data between giving and earning is not just one-way. People do give more when they become richer—research has shown that a 10 percent increase in income stimulates giving by about 7 percent—but people also grow wealthier when they give more.[24]*

Professor Brooks' article goes on to share results from research conducted by the Center on Philanthropy at Indiana University which revealed that "in 2004, $100 in extra income per American drove about $1.47 in addition charitable giving," and "… $100 in giving stimulated more than $1,800 in increased G.D.P."[25]

So, on those days when momentum is hard to come by, simply remember that each time you are generous with your time, treasure, and talent, you are improving your own health and the economic status of your community and country. Not bad for following your passion and doing what you can, with what you have, where you are.

Now that you're equipped for any negative feedback, let's take a look at momentum squasher number two.

Momentum Squasher #2: Personal Distractions

Though I can access focus on a dime, I can also become easily distracted by shiny, new, exciting opportunities. Besides just a few areas, namely taxidermy, anything to do with my internal organs, and renaissance festivals, just about everything interests or intrigues me. I love to learn, and this is an asset, to be sure. At the same time, I can be on one track, gaining steam and making good headway, only to allow myself to be glancing over at the other train and wondering where it's going.

To help me when I get overzealous, I apply a rule from an earlier chapter: not now but soon! This way, while I am working on an initiative that will require, say, two or three years of my time, treasure, and talent, I can know that the new opportunity presented to me will be its follow-up. If I thought I couldn't be involved in the shiny, bright, new opportunity, I would find a way to distract myself and head in its direction. Knowing that it's on my path, but in due time, helps to keep me focused on the task at hand.

My colleague Patty is similar. Here are her distractions and the solutions that had her feeling more fulfilled and more effective.

Patty

Patty likes to call herself a walking example of a distracted person. She has a range of interests from sailing to cooking, fine arts to sculpture, and travel to fashion, to name a few. Patty likes to dabble in each but didn't necessarily become an expert or a connoisseur.

With a mind that raced quickly, she easily becomes distracted by a new hobby, primarily because of its newness.

When it came to her history of charitable work, Patty followed a similar course. She has served on boards of directors for organizations working to cure cancer, reduce incidents of juvenile diabetes, eliminate poverty, ensure health care for all, and end trafficking of women and girls. She always served out her volunteer tenure but, shortly after, would get pulled in by a cause that piqued her interest and felt compelling and important to support.

Patty's range of personal and charitable interests reflect her curiosity, inquisitiveness, and enthusiasm for learning new things. The upside of Patty's range of interests is that she brings zeal and passion to whatever she gets involved in. The downside is that she finds herself jumping from cause to cause. She said yes too often, spreads herself too thin, doesn't become an expert in any one issue, and becomes easily distracted by new causes or organizations she learns about.

According to Webster's dictionary, *distraction* means "to draw or direct (as one's attention) to a different object or in different directions at the same time."

None of us can be our most effective when we are distracted, when we lose focus. This was true for Patty as well.

For her, the key to maintaining momentum is learning to channel her enthusiasm by keeping herself engaged and connected in the work long after the newness wears off. Patty finds that she can't just review financials or make sure the organization was meeting its bylaws. She is content doing this some of the time, but when she does it all the time, she finds herself getting distracted and reading more about the causes her friends are involved in.

Distraction is a momentum squasher. When our mind roams to another cause, we imagine meeting new people, learning new things, and attending new events. Or even if we do stay committed to our cause, life can become a distraction. Imagine a project you've needed to do around your house or apartment. You look at it a lot. You know you should do it. Somehow you find a movie you've been wanting to see, a magazine you can't wait to read, a friend you've lost touch with.

Though working your Generosity Plan is not equivalent to painting a room that needs a fresh coat, you will find that along the way you will get distracted by a whole range of things, from life to other causes.

For Patty, the antidote is to engage her personal passions in her charitable work. After the early magic of the new endeavor wears off for her—as she knows it will—Patty realizes she can use her love of food and cooking to host a dinner fundraiser for the organization. She feels excited to be making food for potential new supporters. Plus, Patty loves to see the spark in the eyes of people just learning about the organization. It reminds her why she got involved and helps her to recapture the early magic of the organization.

At one dinner, Patty was asked to tell her story of how she came to get involved with that cause. She shared her passion for the issue and her desire to make a difference. She also shared about her "scattered" mind and how in the past she had gotten easily distracted with new causes. Then she told the group of dinner guests that seeing the organization through their eyes was a reminder of what brought her to the work. She thanked them for helping her see the value of getting and staying involved.

What are your distractions?

Think about when you have started a new endeavor. Were you unable to follow through as you hoped because you got distracted or bored? Did work demands increase? Did your home life demand more of you? Were you able to talk yourself out of something because it wasn't a requirement and you were fatigued from your day? Do your kids require a lot of you, which has you putting your own needs last? What steps did you take to make sure you did what you needed to do? What worked for you? How could these same tools work if you find yourself getting distracted from meeting your Generosity Plan goals?

You may be like Patty and get distracted because a new cause seems interesting or you see it as an opportunity to learn. If so, what steps can you take to follow through on your Generosity Plan before you move toward a new charitable effort? How can you use the tools and suggestions in this book to keep you on track?

Momentum can be difficult to maintain when the newness wears off. When we first start volunteering, we are excited, glad to be involved, and hopeful about what our contributions can bring. Then, once we've volunteered for a while, though it is still meaningful and important, it can begin to feel monotonous. We talk to the volunteer coordinator because we need to change our schedule. We try to fit in the dentist, a client meeting, a grocery store run on a day we are volunteering. One volunteer shift isn't as exciting as the prior shifts, and we wonder if we're still making a difference.

All of a sudden, what began as a something new and exciting has become a regular part of our schedule. It loses a little bit of its early glamour. When this happens, it can be easy to be swayed to a new volunteer position.

Remember that getting distracted is a normal part of the process. Sometimes being distracted from meeting our goals means we have to revisit and reinvigorate how we are involved, like Patty did. Other times, distraction means we may be feeling a little burned out, and need to cut back on our giving to take a short break and come back feeling renewed and refreshed.

What's most important is that you become aware when distractions are presenting themselves and think about how you can jump those hurdles. Think about your five keys to a successful Generosity Plan. Revisit your vision. Do something bold. Be sure that what you are involved in is still true to your spirit. Get support from friends. Or, as will be described in chapter 10, if you feel you are getting completely off track and know you need a structure in place, start or join a Generosity Club. When you know what causes you to get distracted, you will be able to deal with it head on.

What should you do if you find that after taking all the steps and measures to stay focused in support of maintaining your momentum, you still feel distracted and unengaged in supporting a certain cause? In this case, it may be that you are ready to complete what you began and, for your own personal growth, you may need to find a new effort to get behind. You won't always stay with one organization or one charitable effort for life. You will expand your involvement, and expansion is great; it fuels momentum. You just want to be sure that your expansion is not based on the hope that the grass is greener on the other side, because you'll find that when you get to the other side, that grass needs to be mowed and cared for just the same as your current backyard.

Final Thoughts on Maintaining Momentum

Do you know the fable of the tortoise and the hare? I used to favor the hare. Okay, I *was* the hare. Turns out that tortoise is one wise little animal.

> *One day, a tortoise and a hare are speaking. The hare laughs at the tortoise for how slow the tortoise moves. The tortoise challenges the hare to a race. The hare laughs and agrees, confident that with his speed he will certainly win.*

On the day of the race, the hare runs speedily from the start-ing point, leaving the tortoise far behind. So confident is the hare that he stops to tell other animals about the silliness of the race. Eventually, he decides to take a nap.

When he awakes, he finds that the race is over. The tortoise—going slow and steady—crossed the finish line. The tortoise won the race.

Twenty-six years ago, when I began my activism, I assumed the persona of the hare. Fast, fast, fast. Go, go, go. However, unlike the hare, I didn't nap. I went and went and went, hoping that if I ran fast enough and quickly enough, I could change the world. At night when I went to sleep, I was plagued with the wrongdoings in the world. I didn't know how to live my life—go to work, spend time with friends, go out to dinner—when at the same exact moment that I was having a good day, countless other people were living in abject poverty, fighting to stay alive in their country's war, battling disease and illness. I became so overwhelmed by what I felt I couldn't do, I experienced a waning spirit, diminished impact, and faltering momentum.

To have true impact, I knew I would need to change my way of being, but I was scared to leave behind the persona of the hare. After all, hadn't that high-octane energy gotten me to this place? How could I be effective if I moved along slowly?

I gained solace and perspective in learning from others who had come before me. Their secret seemed to be in approaching the work with a slow and steady pace. Where at first I was concerned that slow translated into complacency, I soon learned that in order for your cause to benefit, you need to be strong, healthy, well-fed, well-rested, and capable of staying the course.

I began to learn that going at the speed of light eventually resulted in fatigue and burnout. I learned that by going slow and steady, I could circumvent overwhelm and lead instead with resolve and determination. And while slow and steady cannot change the world overnight, it does change the world because it changes your own capacity to be in support of your cause over the course of your life. Our causes will not benefit from us barreling out of the gate and then taking a nap under a tree. Our causes will benefit from us taking one step at a time and doing what we can, with what we have, where we are. No more. No less.

On making social change happen, the great American author and poet Alice Walker said, "This is how change happens. It is a relay race... our job is to do our part of the race, and then we pass it on, and then someone picks it up, and it keeps going. And that is how it is."

Life and gravity are brilliant at helping us to slow down, do our part, and take the route of our friend, the tortoise. For certain, a house fire down the street or a humanitarian crisis in the Democratic Republic of the Congo require fast-moving hares to transmit the urgency, raise awareness, and enact solutions. At the same time, and in both cases, swift action should be followed with a slow and steady rebuilding. Swooping into a problem without a long-term strategy can sometimes cause more harm than good.

In the field of generosity and making a difference, the hare ignites us into action. For this, we love the hare. We love his energy and spunk. After this swift action, the tortoise will be the best guide and friend to your Generosity Plan. The tortoise reminds us to pace ourselves. The tortoise shares with us the importance of the journey and not just the finish line. The tortoise can provide you with the wherewithal to stay the course, exercise patience, and live in the knowledge that your slow and steady contributions will serve the end game far better than swooping in and running to the next challenge.

Here, then, are tried and true methods you can rely on to help you maintain momentum for the long haul:

1. **Create your Future Statement.** Using the box below, write your Generosity Plan Future Statement. What is a Future Statement? Think time capsule. In your mind, jump ahead ten years. How old are you? Where do you live? What are you doing for work? Are you retired? Have you changed fields? Have your children left home? Are your children just born? Take a few moments to visualize you in ten years.

Now, in your Generosity Journal, fill in the responses to these following statements:

- The issue I care about most is ...
- If I had it my way, the biggest change for this issue in ten years will be ...
- When I envision looking back on my life, I would feel I lived a generous and charitable life if I did the following ...

When you need an extra jolt of support or a reminder of why you're doing what you're doing, look to your Future Statement. It will help keep you on track and maintain your momentum.

2. **Be flexible and creative.** When I first started making more than $28,000 per year, I felt ecstatic. I could pay my bills *and* write checks to my favorite nonprofit organizations. I felt like the richest person in the world. Then, I started a company. Starting a company, it turns out, costs quite a bit of money. Now the money that came in the door went straight back into the company versus into the nonprofits I cared so much about. For a few years, I didn't have the resources to write big checks, and I struggled with this. How could I call myself a philanthropist if my giving had decreased? What if I couldn't make a financial gift I had pledged three years ago, when financial resources were more abundant?

The key here: be flexible and creative.

Over the course of your Generosity Plan, you will have financially strong years and leaner years. You will have periods of time on your hands and periods when you can't seem to find a minute to yourself. You might also change careers and no longer be interested in offering your previous skill to your cause.

Like Judy telling her pastor of her church that she would need to modify her giving during her husband's illness, feel free to tell your charity that your life situation has changed but not your commitment. Tell them that while the time, treasure, and talent may be a little less than in past years, you're still there. You're still with them for the long haul. Ask them if there are other ways you could help that would make a difference for them.

I did this with the nonprofits I cared about most. When I had less money to give, I knew I could lean on my time and talents during the leaner financial years. During those years, I gave nonprofit staff free access to my fundraising classes, free access to my materials and toolkits, and free coaching sessions for staff and volunteer leaders. While it wasn't a financial gift, it was a gift they needed in order to be more effective in meeting their mission.

If these are financially lean times for you, what talents and skills can you provide to your charitable effort? Be creative. Be flexible. This approach will likely reveal gifts you didn't know you had and will help you maintain your momentum during all stages of your life.

3. **Resist the urge to swoop in and fix everything.** When we see a wrong, most of us want to make it right. For example, you see a youth center that is run down, lacks good ventilation, and has older furniture that is falling apart. What you envision: an upgraded youth center with ceiling fans, air conditioning for the summer, heating for the winter, sports equipment, reading rooms—a fully equipped facility. Let's say you can write a $1 million check to pay for all the upgrades. Instead of swooping in, you have the opportunity to learn about the center. Ask questions. Do the young people want upgrades? What works best for the community overall? What does the leadership think? What is the plan for training and maintaining upgrades?

4. **Connect to the positive to inspire you.** By creating your Generosity Plan and stepping into the world in the way that matches your vision, objectives, time, treasure, and talent, you are making a difference. As you learn more and get more involved, what can sometimes accompany your journey are feelings of overwhelm, frustration, anger, sadness, or hopelessness. These are completely normal feelings in difficult situations. You should get angry and cry when needed, and most importantly, you should celebrate. Celebrate your involvement. Celebrate the difference you want to make, the difference you are making, and the differences you will make. If your funding helped build a playground in a rural community, visit the playground long after the ribbon-cutting ceremony. Witness the impact of your giving. If you are helping fund education and support for cancer survivors, volunteer at a bike-a-thon to witness the strength and power of the survivors. If you support bringing together grassroots activists for skills building, call the director and ask for success stories. Who or what has been positively impacted as a result of the program? Don't just wait for the newsletter or annual report; reach out to the people who are involved.

Part of my time, treasure, and talent plan includes Chimps, Inc., a chimpanzee sanctuary located in Bend, Oregon. I am happy to give Chimps, Inc. my financial support, free fundraising services, access to my network, and promotion through my e-newsletter. They send me photos, updates, and stories about the chimps, and when I'm able, I visit the sanctuary or I call the director to ask for a story about one of the chimps. On those days when I need an injection of hope and possibility, I remember the quote I read from another donor who supports Chimps, Inc.: "Helping out seven or eight chimpanzees may not mean much, but it means something to the seven or eight chimpanzees."

When you give your time, treasure, and talent, it means something to the cause you care most about. Build in the tools you need to remind yourself of your good work. You will maintain your momentum and, like the tortoise, you will reach the finish line with calm, ease, and effectiveness.

9
Putting It All Together
Your Very Own Generosity Plan

*I*f you have read through this book's first eight chapters and have been keeping notes in a Generosity Journal, you are ready to bring together everything you have learned and get started on your very own Generosity Plan.

In the book's appendix, you will find a summary of each chapter, chapter questions and exercises, and chapter tips. This section will help refresh your memory about the main points of the chapters and their action items. As you are creating your Generosity Plan, look back through your Generosity Journal as well as the book and the appendix to help with your recall and to ensure that your plan includes everything you want it to include.

You can now use your Generosity Journal to map out your Generosity Plan. In your journal, write out one to two sentences in response to the following statements. For best results, follow the sequence below.

- In going back to my giving roots, what I will bring into my current Generosity Plan is ...
- My vision for the world is ...
- My charitable priorities are ...
- The amount of time I want to give to my favorite cause is ...

- The talents I bring that can benefit my cause are ...
- The amount of treasure that I contribute now to charitable organizations is ...
- The treasure I would like to contribute in the coming year in percentage is ...
- When I envision taking a stand within my cause, it looks like ...
- How I will use my voice to express my heart and passion for my cause is ...
- The charities that I am most interested in providing support to are ...
- If I haven't yet chosen my charities, the first step I will take in getting closer to this goal is ...
- When it comes to volunteering, I feel I am already volunteering my time (choose one of the following) formally/informally by ...
- When it comes to volunteering, I want to get more involved in giving my time (choose one or both) formally/informally because ...
- Of the five keys to an effective Generosity Plan, the one that most resonates with me is ...
- The specific action I will take around this one key is ...
- If I find myself becoming distracted from my goals, the one thing I will do right away to maintain my focus is ...
- If someone in my life isn't fully supportive of me moving forward with my Generosity Plan, the tool I will use to maintain my momentum is ...
- If I am interested in joining or starting a Generosity Club (see chapter 10), the value I think it will bring to me is ...
- If I can ask my friends, family members, or coworkers to do one thing to be in support of me creating and living my Generosity Plan, that one thing will be ...

- When I think about the most important reason I am going to create and live my Generosity Plan, the reason that pops up in my head is ...
- For me, what it means to live a generous life is ...

If you have completed most or all of these sentences above, you have created your very own Generosity Plan. Congratulations! As I shared in the introduction of this book, I have met billionaires who were involved in the field of philanthropy and could not complete the above sentences even though they were writing checks for millions of dollars.

As of right now, you are a philanthropist. You have done the work to determine what matters most to you and how you will use your time, treasure, and talent to shape the world. You have turned your intention into action. In doing so, you have become a change agent in the world. As of today, you are being "the change you wish to see in the world." You have decided that *you* are the one you have always been waiting for.

As of today, you will join thousands of other people throughout the world in standing up for what matters most to you. You will do so with a clear and thoughtful plan, one that will allow you to measure your success and celebrate victories. Now, with your commitment to live and lead a more generous life, you can be instrumental in making the world the one we know is possible.

For our children and our children's children, you have stood up and said that each person matters. Each can make a difference.

10
Maximizing Your Impact
Starting a Generosity Club

What's a Generosity Club? It's a gathering of like-minded people, seeking support in their philanthropic efforts. Similar to a book or cooking club, the environment allows for discussion and education into an area many might feel unschooled in.

As mentioned earlier in chapter 1, the group environment of a Generosity Club can help you brainstorm ideas and action plans, giving you the personal support you may need in reaching and maintaining your generosity efforts. The sharing of personal experiences can be key to creating your own Generosity Plan miracles.

Pam

When Pam started creating her Generosity Plan, she felt excited about the possibilities. At the same time, she felt a little overwhelmed and uncertain. She shared that as her plan took greater shape, new questions arose like: What if I start volunteering somewhere and don't like it? Do I complete my time, or do I bow out gracefully? I may not get the bonus this year that I thought I'd get when I wrote my giving budget. How do I still hit my 5 percent without it?

In addition to some of the stumbling block questions, Pam also had ideas for meeting her Generosity Plan goals that she wanted to share and get feedback on. She told her husband about her ideas. She told coworkers. She even told her mail carrier. They were happy for her and encouraged her, but Pam wanted more interaction and more engagement. She wanted someone or some people to be there with her while she worked her plan. "It's not quite a support group I'm looking for. More like a group of people working toward the same goals to bounce ideas off of and share hurdles, successes, struggles, and stories. Who knows? We might even be able to do some charitable work together!"

For Pam, a Generosity Club was born. A Generosity Club is a group of individuals who share similar values and goals coming together in support of meeting those shared goals.

Like book clubs or money clubs, a Generosity Club creates the opportunity for you to network with like-minded individuals, share your best ideas, dismantle hurdles, exchange tips and strategies for success, and in some cases, combine your time, treasures, and talents toward one agreed-upon charitable effort. After examining the added value of a Generosity Club, Pam knew that this was the right approach for her. While she would implement her Generosity Plan goals month by month on her own time, a club would help her stay on track and hold her accountable to her goals.

How do you know if you, like Pam, would benefit from a Generosity Club? Would meeting up with other like-minded individuals make a difference to your Generosity Plan, or is a club not a necessary tool for you in meeting your goals?

The answer to these questions relies on how you profile when it comes to setting goals and meeting them. Some of us are self-starters who read and learn everything we need to know, make decisions, then move forward unhesitatingly on those decisions. Others are connectors who thrive on regular and ongoing conversations and who benefit from group settings and being accountable to members of a group. For the former, a Generosity Club may be interesting but might not be necessary to achieve goals. For the latter, a Generosity Club may be just the right element for success.

Regardless of how you profile, one of the reasons I recommend that you look into a Generosity Club—in addition to its benefits to your thinking about generosity, charity, change, and making a difference—is the interaction with individuals who share your values yet bring different perspectives. In this type of atmosphere, you will experience growth and enrichment. You will likely learn new ideas about how to benefit your cause from other members in the club. You may also meet someone with whom you share a favorite cause and, if you decide to work together, could end up doubling your efforts. Equally important, you may bring a point of view, a new idea, or advice about giving time or resources that provides just the breakthrough for another member.

Additionally, Generosity Clubs ensure that while charity begins at home, it doesn't end there. The issues we face are challenging. The solutions require all of our best thinking. While we won't always love what one another has to say, if we're really listening, we'll likely learn something we did not know. That something could be a key component of our most successful Generosity Plan.

Do you need to belong to a Generosity Club if you work better alone, are a self-starter, or you and your family have created your own Generosity Club? You don't, but remember that the more people you talk to, the more you learn. The more you learn, the more skills you gain. The more skills you gain, the more proficient you will become in making a difference.

If you will mostly work your Generosity Plan solo, remember to refer back to chapter 7 for the five effective keys. These will help you maintain momentum and provide you with tools and tips to keep yourself going.

Generosity Club Profiles

If you've ever been a part of or heard of a book club or money club, then you already have a good idea of how a Generosity Club works and could benefit you. And like book and money clubs, Generosity Clubs vary in size, structure, and goals. Below is a brief overview of three popular clubs—book, investment, and debt free—and a profile of individuals who belong to each. While you're reading these profiles, think about which person you most closely relate to: Jess, Mike, or Liz.

Jess: Book Clubs

Jess loved to read. She read several books per month but found herself missing the chance to talk through books like she did when she was enrolled in college. She thought about taking a literature class to be able to share and exchange her ideas, but with her full-time schedule, she did not want to add classwork, exams, and tests to her life. Jess looked into several local book clubs but either didn't like the genre or couldn't make the times work.

Jess then looked into online book clubs after friends raved about them to her. They said the selections and varieties of clubs were wider than any local, in-person club they could find. Her friends loved being members of several types of clubs, including mystery, literature, blockbuster fiction, and self-help. They touted the convenience, stating that if you hadn't read the book, you could still "sit in" on the discussion, which was helpful before you began reading. They also loved having access to the wide range of views without ever having to leave home after a long day at work.

Jess was sold. She went to the recommended sites, learned the rules of participation, joined, and got started. However, Jess found she didn't get as engaged as her friends did. While she loved reading comments, thoughts, and ideas from people across the United States and beyond, she didn't love spending so much time on a computer. Her day job had Jess sitting in front of a monitor for seven or eight hours a day. Getting home and logging on to a computer was not exactly what she was looking to do in her spare time. She also found that her eyes got tired, and she felt overwhelmed by all the comments and feedback. She even felt a little anxious when she hadn't been online for a bit and needed to catch up on what she had missed. Her first solution was to reduce the number of online book clubs she participated in, which helped ease her stress of not feeling caught up, but she still felt something was missing.

The something that was missing for Jess was the one-on-one, in-person interactions and connections. Jess recognized that, while she didn't love exams and tests in college, she *did* love sitting in a room with other students and hearing them talk about the book, asking questions, walking, and talking after class. She liked being in-person while learning.

When she recognized this need to have community and interpersonal connection, Jess decided to pull back from the online clubs and seek out or start her own informal, in-person book club. Though she knew she would miss the diversity of online clubs, she realized that part of seeking a book club was not just about the books but about creating a community, meeting new people, and really knowing her neighbors.

It took a little searching, but Jess soon found a new book club geared toward readers of fiction. The group began as four members who agreed to meet once a month at a member's house or a coffee shop. Because it was a small group, each member got to choose a selection and then led the group through that discussion. In short time, the group grew to eight and agreed to keep it at this number. While it was a little work for the group to agree on a location each month and for each member to take on a responsibility to make the group work, for Jess, the benefits far outweighed the extra efforts.

Mike: Investment Club

Mike was invited to an investment club meeting by a friend who seemed to have luck in managing and growing finances. He was wary about pooling his financial resources with individuals he hadn't met, but he knew he needed the expertise and thought trying out the investment club could be a useful tool in managing and growing investments.

Right away, Mike liked the educational aspect of the group. While he had read a lot of materials online and subscribed to magazines about finance, he felt that after just two meetings, he had learned more than he had during his efforts going it alone in the six months prior. He also grew to like the idea of pooling his money with the other members. This opened up a new playing field in investing that he could never have achieved on his own. He got smarter about what to read and what not to read, how to read between the lines, how to gauge a realistic return on investment, and how to avoid pitfalls made by first-time investors. The club provided a strong sense of focus and direction that Mike did not have when he attempted to begin investing on his own.

As a member of the investment club, Mike could take the risk with the group and the return could potentially be bigger because of the risk. He put in the amount he was capable of, knowing that some members put in more and some put in less. He didn't see great returns in the beginning, but as he stuck it out, he began to see slightly higher returns. When he reviewed investing materials, he realized that he had made more money with the investment club than he would have made as a solitary investor.

For Mike, an investment club was the right choice. He believed in pooling knowledge and resources toward a shared goal, and he was willing to take a risk. At the same time, he felt more confident knowing that he was taking a risk with a group. He liked the idea of shared investing and accountability, and getting back what he put in.

Liz: Debt-Free Club

Liz belonged to an online debt-free club. The goal of this club was for members to remove debt from their life and take steps toward living a debt-free life.

At first, Liz was anxious about joining the group. She felt she had too much debt. She imagined that others who joined the online debt-free club had a few credit cards or perhaps had gone over the limit one too many times on a store charge card. Because of this, she wondered if the program was geared toward her. She had tried figuring out how to get out of debt on her own but could only make minimum payments on her credit cards and loans so far. Liz was ready for a change.

Because of her shame around her debt, Liz wasn't interested in meeting up in living rooms and laying out her money challenges to a group of strangers. A more private person, Liz sought support, guidance, and encouragement in a more anonymous setting, and she felt the online approach would be the right match for her needs and her personality.

Liz read the stories of people who had started the ninety-day program and felt reassured that they, too, had once felt as she did. Finally feeling good about sharing her debt story with others and getting support, it suited her that she could be online, maintain her privacy, and still receive the benefits from others who had graduated from the program and were now living a debt-free life. There were also others who had experienced setbacks and struggles along the way. Through the program, Liz felt she got what she needed to make the changes she couldn't seem to make on her own: smart, supportive, encouraging advice from people who were seeking the same aim from those who had achieved it. She loved the range of tips she received, and she appreciated the anonymity and convenience of an online experience.

One difficultly for Liz, though, was not having a person she knew to be accountable to. She knew her lack of accountability to herself about her money had gotten her into heavy debt. This way of operating made itself most evident early on in the program. When Liz reached day six, she realized she hadn't fully completed day five's exercises. She shrugged it off and noted to herself how "good" she had been thus far, saying that not completing all of the exercises certainly wouldn't hold her back. She then proceeded to work on day six's exercises and realized that she really did have to complete day five in order to take the next step. Liz felt frustrated and thought to shut her laptop. After all, she hadn't been spending, she was removing clutter from her life, and she was logging on every day. Didn't that count for something?

Liz decided to confide in her good friend Stacy that she had enrolled in this program. Stacy was thrilled she was doing so and offered her help. When Liz told her about wanting to skip over the exercises and get to the parts when she would learn how to spend less, Stacy laughed and told her that skipping over the tough stuff was what got Liz into this situation in the first place. Stacy said that Liz never asked for help and always tried to shoulder things on her own. She said that Liz should fully invest in this program if she was serious about getting out of debt for good. This meant to trust the debt-free instructors, the graduates, and the coursework.

Liz didn't love the suggestion, but she knew her friend and the online club were right. The next day, her friend called and asked, "Did you complete your exercises for the day?" Liz hadn't yet done so but got on it right away.

Liz loved the online program and realized she needed a person to whom she was accountable. Otherwise she could easily lose momentum and not keep to her plan. While the online forum suited her overall personality, needs, and goals, a little help from a good friend made the program the success she hoped it would be.

As you read the stories of Jess, Mike, and Liz, which personality type best resonated with you? Are you like Jess, looking for community connection and one-on-one interaction without a formal or legal structure? Are you like Mike, seeking to maximize the impact of your goals by pooling with others? Or are you like Liz, wanting to learn from others but preferring e-learning because of privacy, anonymity, or lack of time?

Like other clubs, Generosity Clubs come in all shapes and sizes. Your club can be:

- Members who each care about a different cause and who come together for new ideas, support, and encouragement, and as a way to maintain your momentum

- Members who each care about the same cause and want to talk about volunteering time toward a shared goal or pooling financial resources to share with favorite organizations or charitable efforts
- Your immediate or extended family which has a shared charitable goal, or where each member talks about and gains support for the cause nearest to them
- An online presence where you log in to share your successes, ask questions, and seek guidance. Your e-generosity can also be a place where you learn about other Generosity Plans to help add spice and flavor to yours

To help with your thinking about what type of learning and sharing environment is best for you, take a look at these three types of Generosity Clubs: informal, formal, and e-Generosity.

Types of Generosity Clubs

/. **Informal.** A casual Generosity Club is a group of friends or like-minded people who get together to give and get support for their Generosity Plans. Members may support different causes and have different goals. Casual Generosity Clubs tend not to volunteer together or pool financial resources in support of a charity. Rather, informal Generosity Clubs provide a fun and easygoing environment for the exchange of ideas, support, and guidance. Casual groups can meet once a month or more and can choose a range of locations: a member's home, restaurant, coffee shop, internet café, or wine bar. Members pay their own way financially. The contribution of time and best thinking in support of another member's Generosity Plan is the commitment made in a casual Generosity Club. While one person will facilitate discussion, this job is generally to keep each member on time (five minutes to update, five minutes for feedback).

2. **Structured.** A formally structured Generosity Club contains a set number of members who agree to pool their time, talents, and/or treasure to support a shared cause or goal. For example, you and five friends realize that you share a passion for ending childhood hunger. You may have been giving to a local food pantry separately and have talked about the issue, but feel you might be able to make a bigger impact if you learn more and work together as a group. A formal Generosity Club can help you achieve this. While you have your own Generosity Plan for yourself and/or your family, the aspect of your Generosity Plan on hunger relief can be achieved through your Generosity Club's efforts.

As a club, you would agree to your club's vision, mission, and priorities and would create strategies for combining your time, treasure, talent, and taking a stand to have the greatest impact. For example, six members come together to talk about doing their part to help feed hungry children in their county. One member takes leadership on reaching out to the food pantry to gather information and determine the food pantry's greatest needs. Another member agrees to open his home for the first three meetings.

As a club, you needn't have a legal structure. Your commitment is to one another and the charity you have in common. If, however, your club would prefer to have a legal structure in place, there are a range of tools available to you that can be found in the resources section of this book.

3. **E-Generosity.** E-Generosity allows you to take advantage of internet-based technology to share ideas, learn from others, gain inspiration, and maintain momentum. Through e-generosity (the generosityplan.com) you can post your Generosity Plan's vision and strategic goals and even share the first steps you are taking to get underway. You can invite feedback and support from others who are part of the e-generosity community, and you can review others' goals, priorities, and strategies as a way to deepen your own Generosity

Plan. You can post successes on your very own generosity page, including photos of you at work in the community. Of course, if you have created an informal or formal club, your group can also have an e-generosity presence as a way to share what you've learned in support of others who will be launching clubs like yours.

The e-generosity community is available to you if you don't have time for a club but benefit from learning, connecting, and sharing. You may also end up finding other people whose Generosity Plan goals mirror your goals and, through this connection, have an e-generosity buddy with whom you can share your generosity journey.

E-Generosity is not a way to raise money for your cause but a way to exchange ideas and thinking and to showcase what works when it comes to making a difference.

As with other clubs or gatherings, there are advantages to Generosity Clubs, as discussed above, there are also disadvantages. It can only help you to take time to evaluate the challenges associated with starting or joining a Generosity Club. These challenges needn't dissuade you. Instead, in knowing the challenges you could encounter, you will be better prepared to effectively lead or participate in a Generosity Club.

Cons: Informal Clubs

The downside of informal clubs can be the lack of quantifiable and noticeable results. Since it may be a group of friends who create an informal club it can be easy to slip into conversation not related to the goals of your Generosity Club. You may be excited to see friends in a social environment and use much of the time catching up and hanging out. This is okay, especially if one of the goals of your informal club is to build relationships and community. However, the con is that you may feel less progress on your Generosity Plan goals. You may find that four or five meetings have passed and because the group isn't setting goals for the next meeting, you don't get to your plan in between meetings. A solution to this is add extra time at the end of your club's gathering to talk about everything but your Generosity Plan. Just be sure to set aside the time to meet your goals to ensure you hit your own targets and stay on track.

Cons: Structured Club

The greatest cons of a more structured club of any kind emerge around managing groups and sharing the workload.

If, for example, you are starting or joining a club in which members are pooling time or treasure toward a shared cause, you may find that you are more restricted in choosing the volunteer site or the recipient of the funds. When you function alone, you can choose to give your time, treasure, and talent to any place of your choosing. However, when you agree to function in a group atmosphere and to consensus, you may not get the charity of your choosing.

Before joining a structured club, you should ask yourself if your goals are to pool resources for a joint project. If yes, then proceed by asking good questions about decision-making processes and permission to dissent. The structured model may be just right for you. You can make this model even more effective by making sure its approach to making a difference is the approach you are seeking.

You could also find—in either an informal or a structured club— that some members don't do their part. Some members may show up for meetings but not raise their hand when tasks are assigned. They may say they are busy and can't take on extra duties. This could mean that you or other members shoulder responsibilities like researching charities and reporting back to the group. Or a member may not show up for a volunteer project, citing prior commitments or a packed schedule. You may also have a member who takes more than his share of time in group sharing or one who doesn't provide feedback but strongly asserts her need to get feedback. Or a member may be doing his or her fair share, but you find you just plain don't like him; his personality or way of interacting rubs you the wrong way. It could be so distracting that you find you don't enjoy the Generosity Club experience and you consider leaving the group.

Again, what's most important in starting or seeking out a Generosity Club is to know your reason for doing so. What are your goals? Why are you a member?

If you join a club with great enthusiasm then find that not all members are contributing equally, you will not likely be able to change that member or members. While you may feel the urge to rally the other members to remove the less active member, remember you are in the Generosity Club to make a difference and to learn new ways of living a generous and charitable life. Be charitable. Keep your commitments. Show up for the meetings. Participate. Listen. Provide feedback. Agree to facilitate a meeting. Share your best thinking and ideas.

If, after these efforts, you find you aren't getting what you need, it's okay to move on and find a group that better suits your needs and personality. My best advice: do your best and don't get involved with trying to oust a member. If it's not working for you even after you've kept your commitment, simply move on and find the group that is a better fit for you. This approach will help keep you focused on the task at hand: living your Generosity Plan in support of the cause dear to your heart.

Cons: E-Generosity

Since e-generosity meets via the web, you won't experience the same group dynamics that emerge with in-person Generosity Clubs. At the same time, while e-generosity is a convenient forum for sharing ideas, learning about others' efforts, and becoming connected to a wide range of people, it lacks the in-person connection provided by traditional Generosity Clubs.

If you are seeking to meet new people in your town, community, city, or county, e-generosity may not be the right match for you. While the internet and social networking sites have opened up new worlds and new possibilities for people around the globe like never before, some people don't feel the same lift from internet-based associations that they do with in-person connections.

What should you do if your community doesn't have a traditional Generosity Club and you don't have the time or capacity to start one of your own? My best advice is to start with an e-Generosity Club. You may find you can get what you need from interacting on the Generosity Plan's social networking site. Or ask a friend to serve as a additional support and sounding board for you. Your friend needn't have a Generosity Plan of her own. This way, you will still get the benefit of connecting one-on-one and, in time, you may find the drive to start or a join your very own club.

Starting a Generosity Club

If, after reviewing the types of Generosity Clubs, you are most interested in creating an informal or structured Generosity Club, here is a guide to help get you started. Remember to start small, knowing you can grow in time.

Step 1: Determine if any clubs exist in your area.
Before you begin the process of launching your own Generosity Club, do a little research to learn if there is an existing Generosity Club in your area that matches your needs and interests. Ask friends, conduct an online search, or visit

thegenerosityplan.com. You might find a club that has recently begun and is welcoming new members. Or you might find that no club exists yet, but there are individuals interested in getting a club together. If you do find a club and it has already established its aim and goals—and those are a fit for you—you will have far less work ahead of you. If you find other individuals interested in starting a club and you all share similar hopes, you can start the club with others and delegate responsibility. Or you may find that no existing clubs match your aims or that no one in your area is yet putting out feelers to join a club. That's okay. The important part of this step is that you take the time to learn what is out there.

Step 2: Determine the goals of your club.
Before you can begin recruiting members for a Generosity Club, you will want to name what your purpose is in creating this club and what the club goals are. In short, why are you starting a Generosity Club?

The *why* will help potential club members know if this club is right for them. If, for example, you state to friends or coworkers, "I'm starting a Generosity Club to learn what others are doing charitably," you will likely attract members who are in the thinking phase, are reevaluating their giving, or are looking to informally talk with people about the possibilities around giving. On the other hand, if you state, "I'm starting a Generosity Club to gain support in creating my Generosity Plan and being accountable to my goals. I'm looking to connect with five or six others like me to share ideas and offer guidance and encouragement in meeting our individual Generosity Plan goals," you will likely attract members who are ready to get started and who are looking for a structured network to enable their success and support others.

Ask yourself: Why do I want to start a Generosity Club? What are my aims? My goals? What do I think will be the value of this Generosity Club? Why do I think this is the right tool for me?

As with all the questions and exercises in this book, there is no wrong answer. You may want to start or join a club for its social component. You may want a club so you can get serious with your plan and meet your deadlines and goals. You may want to start or join a club to pool resources with others and maximize your impact. Take the time to determine why you want to start a club and what you hope the benefits of this club will be.

Step 3: Recruit club members.
Now that you are clear about why you are starting a Generosity Club, your next step is to recruit club members. Think about how many people you'd like to have as members. The size of the club will vary depending on its goals and where members meet.

My recommendation is to start with a small group and then grow in size as the group forms itself. Because a Generosity Club may be a new venue for all members, it could be cumbersome to start, say, a twenty-person club. While the range and diversity of opinions would certainly add value, facilitating a twenty-person club is a lot of work. You could find yourself managing (logistics, locations, cancellations, drop-outs, drop-ins) versus participating in the club. You could, of course, rotate meeting facilitators and locations to ensure that duties are spread out. This is an effective tool. But remember the why of creating this club and recruit the number of members who can best serve that purpose.

Once you have an idea of how many members will be in your club and you've recruited by word-of-mouth, emails, or flyers, your group will be ready to convene. At your first gathering, you should lead the group into setting guidelines.

Step 4: Set club guidelines.
Once you've brought together the core people in your Generosity Club, take some time for introductions (even if you all know one another). During the introduction, ask each person to answer the following questions: Why was I a yes to joining this Generosity Club? What do I hope I will get out of this experience?

Answering these two questions will help each member connect to the other members of the group. It will help set a tone for the club and will also be useful to know each person's goals, aims, and hopes when your club sets its guidelines.

As a group, consider posing and replying to the following questions. Having agreements about these questions will help avoid misunderstandings and make for a better experience for each member and the club as a whole. An example of an answer to each question is also provided:

- *What is the primary purpose of our Generosity Club?* The primary purpose of the Louisville Generosity Club is to provide support, learn and share ideas, and help club members meet their goals of giving back and maing a difference.
- *As we progress, how will we know we are meeting our goals?* We will know we are meeting our goals if members keep coming back to meetings because they feel meeting time is well spent. We will also know we are meeting our goals if members feel they are more effective in giving their time,

treasure, and talent to their charitable effort because of their participation in this club.

- *How often would we like to meet?* The Louisville Generosity Club will meet the third Thursday of every month from 6 to 8 PM.

- *Where should our meetings be?* Each member will host the meeting at her apartment or home but will not be responsible for paying for or providing food and beverages. Members can bring food and beverages for themselves and other group members if they so desire. The member hosting the event can also choose a different location, like a restaurant, coffee shop, or community center, providing all members agree that a public location is acceptable for meetings.

- *What is our membership minimum and maximum?* We are a Generosity Club provided we have at least two members but no more than eight. If others in the community want to join and we are at our maximum of eight, we are happy to help them start another Generosity Club, giving them the tools we used to launch our own. We also encourage meeting up with other Generosity Clubs if they are interested and our members feel they have the time.

- *How will we decide the topics for each meeting?* For our first three meetings, we will allow the topic discussion to be open, as we are new to Generosity Planning. At the end of the third meeting, we will discuss as a group three areas that we could all benefit from, and agree to cover those topics at the next three meetings. Members are welcome to research these topics to stimulate discussion and thinking.

- *What is the best way for us to ensure shared learning? How much time does each person have to talk about her plan and ask for advice and support?* Our meeting format will allow each member to share her plan and pose questions or seek advice. Each member will have a total of fifteen minutes during the meeting. The member can use that fifteen minutes to update, or he/she can split the time for update and question and answer. No member should discourage another member from seeking his or her goals. Members should only provide feedback when it is requested and if offering constructive advice or support.

- *Do you have to attend each meeting to be a member?* Members are encouraged to attend each meeting to ensure that the club meets its goals and that each member gets the support she needs. We agree that members should attend eight or nine of the meetings in a calendar year. If a member cannot make that commitment, we ask that he/she relinquish his/her seat to a prospective member who can attend at least eight meetings in a year.

  In the case that the Club does not seem to be meeting its primary purpose and aim, the club can disband. Members can then join another club or start a new club. The club is not a legal structure; it is merely a gathering of people who share similar values and are looking to live and lead generous lives. If the club doesn't work out, there are no hard feelings or faults.

Now that you've established your purpose, have a solid membership base, and have determined your goals as a club, you are ready to get down to the business of making your Generosity Plans work.

Step 5: Create the right discussions.
In your Generosity Club, you have the opportunity to create the discussions that are just right for the club members.

Some clubs, like the example above, start out with general discussions to get a feel for what members are thinking and feeling, and what members need so they can be successful in their efforts. Then, once the group has a greater sense of where the needs are, each member can take the lead on researching a topic and helping run the discussion.

For example, if your club has gathered because you all care about the same issue—lack of medical care for children in your community—you may agree as a club that you want to learn more about how many children are affected. One member can bring in research, and this can be the discussion topic. You can agree that the goal of the discussion will be to learn why children are going without and then to talk about some of the proposed solutions that could make a difference. As a club, you could all agree that you like one particular solution and talk about how you can work together to achieve it. Or one member might like one solution while another member prefers a different one. In the case that you don't work together as a group, you can talk through the support you need to move forward with the solution that best speaks to you.

If your club has gathered because you are good friends who have made a commitment to living a more generous life but all have separate causes, you could choose to increase the whole group's knowledge about charity and giving. One member may bring in an article she read about what others are doing to become more charitable. You can then discuss this reading and each say how you might apply it to your own life.

What's most important is not exactly what you choose to cover in your group meetings but that you agree that the topics you choose are relevant and helpful to the group as a whole and to individual members. You'll want to feel as though your time in the club is well spent and that you are adding real value to your Generosity Plan.

Take a few minutes to write down in your Generosity Journal which type of Generosity Club may be the right match for you. Make a note as to why you think this club type will best serve your needs and goals. Can you think of others who may feel similarly and could be potential members?

A Final Opportunity to Determine if a Generosity Club is Right for You

Still not certain if a Generosity Club is the right route for you and your Generosity Plan? The following are a few self-assessment checklists to determine if a club or shared learning environment is the best match for your personality.

A Generosity Club could be a great tool for you if:

- you feed off other people's ideas as a way to stimulate your own best thinking;
- you tend to be better at making and keeping commitments if you have others you are accountable to;
- you enjoy being part of other people's success;
- you are a good listener;
- you see group disagreements about how to run a club as an opportunity to lead or benefit from witnessing others' leadership;
- you are more confident and successful if you feel there are people who are rooting for you and your plan;
- you are good at listening to a range of opinions but don't feel pressured to act on all advice given to you;

- you believe that social change and making a difference happens best in a community-based environment;
- you enjoy shared learning without tests or exams!

A Generosity Club may not be a needed resource for you if:

- you feel you can't fit one more commitment into your schedule;
- you travel a lot and aren't home enough to be able to regularly make meetings or support the group in achieving its goals;
- you and your family have created a family Generosity Plan and prefer for your club to be just the family;
- you feel focused on your Generosity Plan, you know what you need to do and how you need to do it, and you don't require external motivation to keep you going;
- you don't really benefit from a group learning environment. (in school, you didn't join study groups or weren't that interested in group learning activities);
- you're not a social person by nature, and joining a club would likely cause more anxiety than provide ease and comfort.

Questions to ask before starting or joining a Generosity Club:

- What are my expectations of this club?
- What do I want a Generosity Club to provide for me?
- What specific ways do I think a Generosity Club could benefit me?
- What kind of commitment am I willing to make to ensure a successful Generosity Club?
- What am I not willing to do?
- Do I have any reservations about joining a Generosity Club?
- What will I consider a successful Generosity Club experience?

Take time to make notes about Generosity Clubs in your journal. Think about how a club may benefit your thinking and the goals of your plan. Could a Generosity Club be just the right tool for your success?

Clubs of all sorts are a global phenomenon. People from all walks of life join clubs for support, encouragement, motivation, tips, and accountability. Groups like book, money, and investment clubs have taken off in size and scope and have proven to be an effective vehicle, as have clubs for weight loss, running, or cycling, and groups like Alcoholics Anonymous and Narcotics Anonymous. Like all of these associations, Generosity Clubs have the power to transform thinking into action in support of making a lasting difference in the world and your own life. Think of a Generosity Club as a powerful resource to give you the advice, encouragement, and support you need to fully live your generous life.

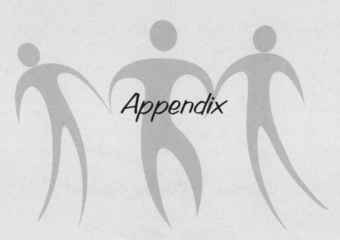

Appendix

Introduction

Summary

When you hear the word *philanthropy*, what image comes to mind? The word philanthropy derives from the Greek word *philanthropos*, which means "humanity, benevolence, or loving of humankind." While *generosity* is "the habit of giving," *leading with generosity* is the "habit of giving, especially when it feels out of your comfort zone, a little nerve-wracking, and down right terrifying."

Philanthropy and generosity look like:

- African-Americans building churches and universities just one hundred years after being brought to the United States as slaves.
- A small, quiet community exposing the dangers of a power plant and each community member giving time, talent, and treasure to make a difference.
- Women in post-genocide Rwanda pooling their dollars to buy school uniforms for their children, generators for their villages, and bulk food to benefit the greater good.

- Neighbors helping a man who might lose his home from a subprime housing loan.
- The Cherokee Nation donating $3 million to the Oklahoma school system.
- A community coming together to make sure that a neighbor's sick child can afford medical care and treatment.
- You giving "what you can, with what you have, where you are."

Chapter 1: Getting Started

Chapter Summary

Much like tracing ancestry, reconnecting with your giving traditions will create continuity in your philanthropic efforts. You will remember what you loved about making a difference. You will recall the good feelings that came with knowing you were doing something that helped someone in need. You will remember the part of you that gave without expectation of return. You will reconnect to being fulfilled by what you *could* do rather than worrying about what you couldn't do. You will likely uncover that you were involved in charitable work far earlier in your life than you initially thought.

Chapter Questions and Exercises

1. What do I remember about giving in my family? Did my parents or guardians volunteer? Did we talk about those in need?

2. Did my family encourage giving back? In what way? Through faith-based activities, school, community groups?

3. What were attitudes about giving back? Positive? Negative? Neither?

4. Who did I see volunteering or helping out? What was a time when I or someone I knew helped a person or an animal in need? What feelings emerge when I describe the situation?

5. Did I volunteer? If yes, when was the first time? Was I nudged to do it by a parent or teacher? How did I feel about it? How do I feel about it now?

6. Outside of your parents and siblings, who were your other relatives: grandparents, aunts, uncles, cousins? How often did you see them? Can you recall a relative who did something that inspired you?

7. Can you recall an act of kindness from someone in your immediate surroundings who made an impact on you? What was it? What did you feel about it?

To round out chapter 1 exercises, reply to the following in your Generosity Journal:

What one thing can I do today that will make a difference for someone I know or someone I can help but may never meet?

Chapter Tips

List three different acts of your own personal generosity. Chances are very likely that you have given selflessly for the benefit of others. List three different times when you have given to someone without expectation of return. How did you feel when you gave of yourself? What was the impact on the recipient? What do those actions say about you and what you value?

Make a list of individuals who inspire you. Who inspires you? Have you read a story recently about someone whose actions were admirable? Who in the public eye do you look up to? Have you been inspired by a neighbor? A coworker? Whether you are inspired by the works of a great spiritual leader or by the efforts of someone you've met in passing, list out the traits of that individual. Which of these traits do you want to continue to cultivate in you? How can your Generosity Plan support you in living those qualities?

Create a Generosity Club. Like book clubs, money clubs, or investment clubs, Generosity Clubs allow you to share your knowledge and to benefit from others' experiences. The group environment can help you unleash your best thinking, take action, leverage efforts, and get ideas to support you in your generosity efforts.

Chapter 2: If I Ran the World . . .

Chapter Summary

"A vision statement is a vivid, idealized description of a desired outcome that inspires, energizes, and helps you create a mental picture of your target."

—RODGER CONSTANDSE

If going back to your giving roots is the heart of your Generosity Plan, then unlocking your vision is its soul. This step will accomplish multiple goals, guiding you to make the right charitable decisions by clarifying exactly what you care about most and what moves, motivates, and inspires you. By unlocking your personal vision, you will learn to lead and give from a place of hope and possibility rather than from a place of overwhelm or uncertainty. As a result, you will give your time and resources to only those causes about which you are most passionate. This approach will maximize your impact and help you to make the difference you long for and that you are fully capable of making.

Chapter Questions and Exercises

1. What is wrong in the world? What is broken that needs to be fixed? What do I care about most in the world? What matters to me? What keeps me up at night? What gets me out of bed in the morning?

2. Using the tips below, craft your first vision statement. When you read your vision, do you feel hopeful? Do you feel inspired? If you read this vision to others, how do they respond? If you imagine reading this vision to a young person, would you be proud of what you wrote?

3. Look closely at your vision statement. How and through what means do you want to help move that vision to reality?

4. Use your Generosity Journal to list out your priorities. If you need time to discover them, make a list of three to five things you need to do to determine what you'd like to learn (*Are there local groups doing this work? Can people at a community organization, church, or synagogue share with me what they are doing? Which organizations welcome children as volunteers?*).

Sample Vision and Priorities

Use your Generosity Journal to write out your own vision statement and your top priority areas.

Jill's Vision Statement	Jill's Priorities
Children are our most precious resource. The life of a child changes adults into parents and parents into grandparents. Children are our legacy and our hope for a community that we have started to build and that they can make better. I envision a world where all children have healthy food, clean water, and affordable health care, and I envision a world where we have the will to make this possible. That will starts with me.	1. Children's health care: local medical clinics providing direct care and national groups I can trust that work on legislation and provide hands-on opportunities for my daughters and me 2. Clean water: local clean water initiatives and products that reduce waste and promote new initiatives 3. Healthy food: healthy products for my local pantry and support for the WIC (Women, Infants, Children) program

Chapter Tips

Stand for something not against something. If your deepest passion is an end to hunger, instead of saying, "My hope is to see hunger eliminated," write instead, "I envision a world where all people have an abundance of healthy, nutritious food that serves them in their daily life and in meeting their highest potential." Create a vision statement that is hopeful, positive, forward thinking, and that allows you to see possibility.

Be specific. Instead of saying, "I envision a world where everyone gets a good education," write instead, "I envision a world where we all make educating our children a top priority and this is enacted through partnerships in the public and private sectors." Specificity asks you to dig a little deeper and learn about what you want to change and where you think that change should happen.

Repeat this quote to yourself: "Every really new idea looks crazy at first." Now, list out ideas that were once thought to be crazy and that have worked out pretty well (the Earth is round, the end of the seven-day workweek and the birth of the weekend, American women getting the right to vote).

By yourself or with a small group, answer the question: if I ran the world, could I make the changes I wanted, and if there were no limitations, what three things would I implement starting today? These can be large or small. You may say, "make sure every school has enough teachers, computers, and books so that no student goes without" or "ensure that every single person has a job to go to and that there would be another employment opportunity available if someone were laid off." The more you practice saying the big, hopeful, absurdly wonderful statements, the closer you will get to landing on your passion and setting the course for your Generosity Plan.

Take ten. Take all the internal resistances that arise when you begin to envision ("that will never happen" or "my kids will think this is ridiculous"). Put aside negative thoughts. In about ten minutes, you can come back to them if you miss them. Until then, let's just take a ten-minute vacation from their limiting impact on you so you can think from a visionary place. Remember: in your vision, anything is possible and all is achievable.

If you are a parent or grandparent reading this book and want to help your children or grandchildren create a Generosity Plan with the family and/or help them have their own mini-Generosity Plans, here is a tip:

Each family member should create her/his own vision statement. Then, the family should share your responses. By doing this, you will see the threads that connect your giving as a family and the uniqueness that you bring as well. As you progress through this book, you will find ways to give as a family and give separately. In Jill's case, she gives to children's health, and her daughters give a portion of their allowance to a local animal shelter and to an environmental protection group. As a family, they listen and learn about one another's cause, and once every six months, they volunteer at one family member's favorite charitable cause.

Chapter 3: How to Change the World

Chapter Summary

Time: *noun*, a continuous, measurable quantity in which events occur in a sequence proceeding from the past through the present to the future

Treasure: *noun*, stored wealth, or valuable or precious possessions of any kind

Talent: *noun*, natural abilities or qualities

Stand: *verb*, to occupy a place or location

Voice: *noun*, the instrument used to speak

The time, treasure, and talent model works because it combines and leverages all of our gifts in service to the greater good. Together, they can transform money into action, time into outcomes, and talents into possibilities. When we find where we stand in our cause, we feel stronger knowing our unique place and role. When we add our voice, however, we choose to express that voice, we add depth to our experience, and we ensure that our cause is strong and visible.

Chapter Questions and Exercises

1. When you think about contributing your time, treasure, and talent, what opportunities do you see available to you? Where do you get stuck? What creative ways can you think of to help you get unstuck?

2. What does taking a stand mean for you? What if you're not the leader of a social movement or a known figure within a global cause? What does it look like to take a stand if you're working full time? Raising children? Busy getting out of debt? Building a career? Or what if you are a shy or quiet person?

3. Where is the place for you? Where do you want to stand? Think of others you know who take a stand. What about them makes taking that type of stand work?

4. How will you loudly or quietly stand in your cause? What actions would have you feeling that you truly stepped up for your greatest passion?

5. When it comes to your greatest passion, how do you define voice? How do you express your voice for your favorite cause? How can the expression of your voice help you stand within your cause?

6. For you, what does standing in and for your cause and voice have to do with generosity? What are the benefits of taking a stand and expressing your voice as a group versus as one person? What are the opportunities you see that could allow you to express voice and take a stand with others?

Chapter Tips

Be true to your unique voice. If you're a quiet person, be true to your quiet power. If you are a more thunderous personality, be true to your extroverted self. Stand in your unique voice and you will do wonders for your cause.

Call on your friends. When thinking about contributing your gifts, call on your friends and others to help you figure out ways you can get involved, and use your best skills to benefit your favorite cause.

Envision limitlessness. Remove phrases from your vocabulary like "I don't have enough time to get anything done," "I don't have enough money," and "I wish I were more talented." These phrases position you to not fully offer your gifts. Instead, tell yourself you have the exact amount of time you need to achieve all of your goals, enough money to support your life and your causes, and just the right talents to make a difference.

Chapter 4: Choosing Charities

Chapter Summary

Charity—in all its shapes, sizes, and permutations—asks us to be a better person than we were yesterday.

As you get more involved in the cause you care about, you will learn what you need to know to help advance its important work. This learning will open the possibilities of your generosity and help to define how and in what ways you will be charitable, be that in direct aid, social change, or social justice.

Chapter Questions and Exercises

1. For you, what is the value of charity? What does it ask of you? Do you feel you have an obligation to help those in need?

2. What does it mean to be a charitable person? Can you recall a time when you were charitable toward something or someone even though you didn't understand it or him/her? Can you recall a time when you were less than charitable? What opportunities await you today to be charitable?

3. As you think about your charities of choice, what do you already know you are looking for?

4. What other qualities are you seeking when you think about giving your time, treasure, and talent? Do you need to know how an organization is spending the money that is donated? Are you interested in learning how the organization measures success?

5. Answer the following:
- The issue I care about most is ...
- I am most interested in ...

Example: *The issue I care about most is* feeding hungry children. *To support this cause, I am most interested in giving locally to groups that provide direct service. While I don't necessarily have* *to provide hands-on support, I do want to know how the group defines success. I also want to know that the people in charge understand the problems and the best way to solve them.*

Chapter Tips

If you want to know what is happening with your financial contribution, ask. If you want to make sure your time spent will be effective, ask how and in what ways your time contribution will make a difference. If you want to be sure your talents will positively benefit your favorite cause, ask how your talents will do that. For your most effective Generosity Plan, there's no substitution for raising your hand and doing your part to make it work.

Think of charity not as an end-of-the-year activity, but as an act you can practice daily. Opportunities to perform charitable acts present themselves every day. Take advantage of these moments and slow down. Witness where and how you can make a difference in someone's life. This flexing of your charitable muscle will help you get cleaver about which acts bring you meaning and significance, translating into a more fulfilling Generosity Plan.

Chapter 5: Finding the Time to Give Your Time

Chapter Summary

There are two ways to give time: formal and informal.

With the vast and growing nonprofit sector, many of us give our time through formal or structured programs. Formal types of giving time include mentoring a young person, volunteering at a soup kitchen, sorting clothes at a Salvation Army or Goodwill, reading to patients at a hospital or to the elderly in a nursing home.

At the same time, giving your time happens informally every day, all over the world. And, according to statistics, it is women who more often than men give of their time in this way. With formal volunteering, hours contributed get counted and you are most likely helping out strangers. With informal volunteering, hours contributed don't get counted and you are most likely helping out friends, family, neighbors, or coworkers.

Both ways of giving your time matter. If you do one but not the other, you will surely make a difference. However, giving both will help you feel fulfilled and connected in a whole new way as you develop your practice of generosity.

Chapter Questions and Exercises

1. How have you given your time informally? List friends or family members you have helped. Think about how you have helped lift a burden or stress for someone you know. What did you enjoy about this experience? Was there something about the experience you didn't enjoy? Would you repeat the giving of time?

2. How have you given your time formally? List organizations or initiatives you have helped. What did you enjoy about this formal giving? Was there something about the experience you didn't enjoy? Do you want to continue giving time in this way? If you haven't volunteered formally yet, write ideas you've had about giving your time. What do you hope the formal volunteer experience will bring?

3. What would be your ideal volunteer experience? Don't worry if you think you're not qualified. Simply write what your dream volunteer job would be. It can be down the street or halfway around the world. No answer is too big or too small.

Chapter Tips

The key to a successful Generosity Plan is actually enjoying the time you are donating. You must enjoy your volunteer activities in order to keep coming back and to keep making a difference. If you say yes to a task because no one else will do it or you feel you should, you are not giving of your time in the most effective way.

Create a time budget so you can figure out how many hours you have to give. Just like budgeting the money you give that keeps you from draining your bank account down to zero, creating a time budget keeps you from draining *you* down to a puddle of tired.

Use your journal to remember how you have given your time formally and informally, note what has and hasn't worked for you, and document what you hope for in the future. If you'd like to try out a volunteer experience but feel a little nervous, ask a friend or coworker if they'd like to volunteer with you. Giving your time has unlimited application. What's the right volunteer opportunity for you?

Chapter 6: How Much Can You Contribute?

Chapter Summary

Determining just the right amount of your finances to share will help you learn how to more easily and seamlessly make these contributions with minimum overwhelm and maximum joy.

Creating your giving budget based on percentages and not dollar amounts is a smart and empowering way to give.

The average American family gives 3.2 percent of earnings to charitable causes.

Explore giving in uncertain financial times, arming yourself with the tools you need to give to your capacity and desire, no matter the size of your wallet or the state of the economy. Don't stop giving or getting. Stay involved. We need our friends, neighbors, and tribe when circumstances are at their most difficult, and they need us.

Chapter Questions and Exercises

1. How do you define money? What is money's purpose? How do these feelings about money and its purpose impact how you share your money with a good cause?

2. How do you profile when it comes to seeing possibility versus seeing barriers? Do you see hurdles or opportunities?

3. To determine the percentage of your income you have been giving, make a list of groups you know you've written checks to. Do you have an organization you normally give to once or more per year? Do you give to your college? Church? Mosque? Temple?

4. Take stock of your giving from the past year. Are you part of a monthly pledge program in which your credit card is charged $25 each month? Have you recently made a gift in response to an urgent need, like a natural disaster? Have you made a gift to someone involved in a bike-a-thon? Have you recently bought Girl Scout Cookies or raffles? Did you give money to a family member in need?

5. Following question 4, take the amounts—no matter their size—and add them up. This is how much you gave in total in the last year.

Now that you have this number, calculate your current charitable giving as a percentage of your annual income.

6. Following question 5, when you learned your number, what did you think of it? Is it reflective of the portion of your budget you want to allocate to generosity? Is it just about right? Is it lower than you thought? Would you like it to be more but you can't really see how you could increase it, given debts or other obligations?

7. What's truly affordable? What will be the right starting point for you? Would you like to grow your percentage over time? Would you like to put aside money every week? Every month? Do you have a bonus coming this year? Could you allocate a percentage of it now toward your total generosity goal?

8. What kind of support do you need from friends and family to hit your percentage goal? Do you have a friend who you can buddy with to meet your goals? If cash feels tight but you still want to hit a certain goal, can you fundraise for the balance?

Chapter Tips

Be creative when it comes to developing your giving budget. Think about how you can get used to giving a certain percentage of your earnings, and then begin to look at how you can slowly and steadily increase that percentage if an increase is the right match for you. Above all, ensure that your generosity percentage reflects how much you care.

Ask for help from family or friends. If budgeting isn't your strong suit, seek out help from people you know who do it well. Tell them that adding generosity to your life budget is important to you, and ask them to help you meet your goals.

Start with what's affordable. While you may want to give $1,000 to a favorite organization, you may not be able to do that today. Begin with what you can truly afford. From here, you will be able to sustain generosity at this level and (hopefully) grow your giving.

Chapter 7: Position Yourself for Success

Chapter Summary

The five keys to a successful Generosity Plan are: vision, boldness, authenticity, staying the course, and support.

In order to know that you are having success with your Generosity Plan, you have to define what success looks like to you. While some may need to see immediate results stemming from their contributions, others may see the very act of participating as success. Defining success now will help prevent you from feeling like you're not making progress. Instead, doing so will maintain your momentum and help you to know that you are on track.

Chapter Questions and Exercises

1. What does success look like to you? When you've felt successful in the past, why did you feel that way? Was it getting a job or promotion, or was the success in the hours or years you invested to get it?

2. How do you define success?

3. What will it look like to have your Generosity Plan turn out well? In creating your Generosity Plan, what is your desired end?

4. What role can generosity and charity play in your definition of success?

Chapter Tips

Make sure you are connected to your vision. It will carry you through difficult times and remind you why you are involved.

Be bold in the way that you define bold. Imagine stepping out of your comfort zone. How could taking a bold action benefit your efforts?

Staying the course provides great benefit to your cause. When we become ambassadors or advocates of our cause, we are stepping up in support of its short-term and long-term aims. Feel free to expand your interests and horizons, and stay true to the cause that is closest to your heart. It will benefit and so will you.

Chapter 8: Maintaining Momentum

Chapter Summary

Momentum can be difficult to maintain if we, when we start a new endeavor like a Generosity Plan, go too fast at first, don't lead with a plan, or get stopped in our tracks by naysayers and distractions. A Generosity Plan helps you proceed slowly and steadily and gives you the tools to maintain momentum for the long haul, increasing your impact.

Additionally, new studies and research show that giving time and treasure is good for your emotional well-being and your financial stability. Feeling good and feeling financially stable will help you stay the course, knowing that your contributions are not only good for your cause but good for you.

Chapter Questions and Exercises

1. Have you encountered resistance when you've wanted to get more involved in a cause? From whom? How did you respond?

2. Who do you know that will support you getting involved or more involved in an important cause?

3. What distracts you from meeting a goal or a task? What two things can you do when you get distracted that will help you maintain your momentum?

Chapter Tips

Naysayers are the opposite of a support system. Their negative banter about your positive steps can be a drain and could make you doubt your capacity to make a difference. There's no need to engage in debate or to explain yourself or your actions. If they antagonize you, respond with:

- You know, I used to feel the exact same way. Then I created a Generosity Plan, started reading about other people like me making a difference, and realized that if I don't do my part, I'm the weak link in the chain. Alone, I can't do it, but it can't be done without me.

- Before I got more involved, I thought it was the environment or jobs. I really did think they were pitted against each other, but I've since learned differently. It sounds like you still think they are at odds.

- Can you tell me what you're involved in? I'd love to know more about that.

- What do you think we should do about it?

Don't apologize for what you care about most. You are following your heart and your passion. This requires no apologies or explanations.

Choose to surround yourself with people who support you. What does support look like for you? Determine the support you need; be clear about it. Then approach the people who want you to be successful, and pursue your passions. Ask them for specific support, and involve them in your Generosity Plan.

Chapter 9: Putting It All Together

Chapter Summary

You are ready to make your very own Generosity Plan. Congratulations! As of today, you are joining thousands of other people throughout the world in standing up for what matters most to you. You will do so with a clear and thoughtful plan—one that allows you to measure your success and celebrate victories. Because of your commitment to live and lead a generous life, you will leave this world better than you found it.

Chapter Questions and Exercises

In going back to my giving roots, this is what I will bring into my current Generosity Plan:

1. My vision for the world is ...

2. My charitable priorities are ...

3. The amount of time I want to give to my favorite cause is ...

4. The talents I bring that can benefit my cause are ...

5. The amount of treasure that I contribute now to charitable organizations is ...

6. The percentage of treasure I would like to contribute in the coming year is ...

7. When I envision taking a stand within my cause, it looks like ...

8. I will use my voice to express my heart and passion for my cause by ...

9. The charities that I am most interested in providing support to are ...

10. If I haven't yet chosen my charities, the first step I will take in getting closer to this goal is ...

11. When it comes to volunteering, I feel I am already volunteering my time (choose one of the following) formally/informally by ...

12. When it comes to volunteering, I want to get more involved in giving my time (choose one or both) formally/informally because ...

13. Of the five keys to an effective Generosity Plan, the one that most resonates with me is ...

14. The specific action I will take around this one key is ...

15. If I find myself becoming distracted from my goals, the one thing I will do right away to maintain my focus is ...

16. If someone in my life isn't fully supportive of me moving forward with my Generosity Plan, the tool I will use to maintain my momentum is ...

17. If I am interested in joining or starting a Generosity Club, the value I think it will bring to me is ...

18. If I can ask my friends, family members, or coworkers to do one thing to support me in creating and living my Generosity Plan, that one thing would be ...

19. When I think about the most important reason I am going to create and live my Generosity Plan, it is ...

Chapter Tips

Refer to your Generosity Journal to refresh your memory. If you've kept a journal and made notes while reading through each chapter, now is a time it will come in handy. Refer back to it to be sure you include in your plan important details and nuances that will make the plan uniquely yours.

Fill it out with a friend or family member. If you learn better by having someone to talk to, ask a friend or family member to sit with you while you answer the nineteen statements above.

Be specific. Specificity will help you create a plan that calls you to action. Include as much detail in your responses as possible in order to help you to take your first steps.

Chapter 10: Maximizing Your Impact

Chapter Summary

A Generosity Club is a group of individuals who come together in support of meeting shared goals and values. Like book clubs or money clubs, a Generosity Club creates the opportunity for you to network with like-minded individuals, share your best ideas, dismantle hurdles, exchange tips and strategies for success, and in some cases, combine your time, treasures, and talents toward one agreed-upon charitable effort.

Chapter Questions and Exercises

A Generosity Club could be a great tool for you if:

1. You feed off of other people's ideas as a way to stimulate your own best thinking.

2. You tend to be better at making and keeping commitments if you have others you are accountable to.

3 You enjoy being part of other people's success.

4. You are a good listener.

5. You see group disagreements about how to run a club as an opportunity to lead or benefit from witnessing others' leadership.

6. You are more successful if you feel people are rooting for you.

7. You are good at listening to a range of opinions but don't feel pressured to act on all advice given to you.

8. You believe that social change and making a difference happens best in a community-based environment.

9. You enjoy shared learning but without tests or exams!

A Generosity Club may not be a needed resource for you if:

1. You feel you can't fit one more commitment into your schedule.

2. You travel a lot and aren't home enough to be able to regularly make meetings or support the group with achieving its goals.

3. You and your family have created a family Generosity Plan and prefer for your club to be just the family.

4. You feel focused on your Generosity Plan. You know what you need to do and how you need to do it, and you don't require external motivation to keep you going.

5. You don't really benefit from a group learning environment. In school you didn't join study groups or weren't that interested in group learning activities.

6. You're not a social person by nature, and joining a club would likely cause more anxiety than ease and comfort.

Before starting or joining a Generosity Club, ask:

1. What are my expectations of this club?

2. What do I want a Generosity Club to provide for me?

3. What specific ways do I think a Generosity Club could benefit my plan?

4. What kind of commitment am I willing to make to ensure a successful Generosity Club?

5. What am I *not* willing to do?

6. Do I have any reservations about joining a Generosity Club?

7. What will I consider a successful Generosity Club experience?

Chapter Tips

An informal Generosity Club is a group of friends or like-minded people who get together to give and get support for their Generosity Plans. Members may support different causes and have different goals. Casual Generosity Clubs tend to not volunteer together or pool financial resources in support of a charity.

A formal Generosity Club contains a set number of members who agree to pool their time, talents, and/or treasure to support a shared cause or goal.

An e-Generosity community is available to you if you don't have time for an in-person club but benefit from learning, connecting, and sharing. E-Generosity allows you to take advantage of internet-based technology to share ideas, learn from others, gain inspiration, and maintain momentum. Explore thegenerosityplan.com for more information.

As a club, you agree to your club's vision, mission, priorities, and create strategies for combining your time, treasure, talent, and taking a stand to have the greatest impact.

As a club you needn't have a legal structure. Your commitment is to one another and the charity you have in common.

Starting a Generosity Club takes five steps: (1) determine if any clubs exist in your area, (2) determine the goals of your club, (3) recruit club members, (4) set club guidelines, and (5) create the right discussions.

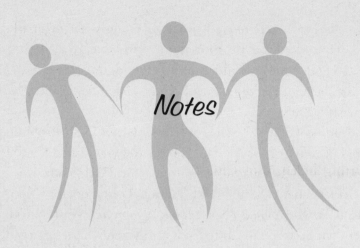

Notes

Introduction

1. *Science of Generosity*, University of Notre Dame Science of Generosity, (2009), http://generosityresearch.nd.edu/.

Chapter 2

2. Eric Allenbaugh, *Deliberate Success: Realize Your Vision with Purpose, Passion, and Performance* (Franklin Lakes, NJ: Career Press, 2002), 27, quoted in Burt Nanus, *Visionary Leadership* (San Francisco: Jossey-Bass, Inc., 1992), 31.

Chapter 3

3. Yvonne M. Brake, "Black Philanthropy," briefing paper, Case Western Reserve University, 2001, http://learningtogive.org/papers/paper6.html (accessed January 2009).

Chapter 4

4. Gwendolyn Mink and Alice O'Connor, *Poverty in the United States: An Encyclopedia of History, Politics, and Policy* (Santa Barbara: ABC-CLIO, 2004), 68.

5. Audits of States, Local Governments, and Non-Profit Organizations, "Circular No. A-133," *Federal Register* (June 27, 2003), 6, http://www.whitehouse.gov/omb/circulars/a133/a133.pdf.

6. Independent Sector and National Center for Nonprofit Boards, *What You Should Know About Nonprofits* (Washington, DC: Independent Sector, 2001), http://www.independentsector.org/PDFs/WhatUShouldKnow.pdf.

7. Independent Sector, "Facts and Figures about Charitable Organizations," March 2009, http://www.independentsector.org/pro grams/research/ Charitable_Fact_Sheet.pdf (accessed February 2009).

8. Better Business Bureau Wise Giving Alliance, "Charitable Donation Tax Deductions," revised 2006, http://www.bbb.org/us/Charity-Tax-Deductions (accessed February 2009).

9. Urban Institute, National Center for Charitable Statistics, "Quick Facts About Nonprofits," 2008, http://urban.org/statistics/quickfacts.efm.

10. Kathleen S. Kelly, PhD, *The Top Five Myths Regarding Non-Profits* (Lafayette: University of Louisiana at Lafayette, 2005), 83.

11. Jan Masaoka, "Alligators in the Sewer: Myths and Urban Legends about Nonprofits," *Board Café* newsletter (San Francisco: Compass Point Nonprofit Services, 2005), 83.

12. Independent Sector and National Center for Nonprofit Boards, *What You Should Know About Nonprofits* (Washington, DC: Independent Sector, 2001), http://www.nonprofitmaine.org/all_about_nonprofits.asp.

13. Ronald L. and Caryl Rae Krannich, *Jobs and Careers with Non-Profit Organizations* (Manassas Park: Impact Publications, 1998), 86.

14. *Who Is CDF?*, Children's Defense Fund, http://www.chil drensdefense.org/who-is-cdf/.

15. *WNY Women's Fund*, Women's Funding Network, http://www.womensfundingnetwork.org/.

16. Why CANDi, Cats and Dogs International, http://www .candiinternational.org/about-candi/why-candi (accessed September 2009).

17. Elizabeth Schwinn, "Many Americans Say Charity Overhead Costs Are Too High, Study Finds," *The Chronicle of Philanthropy* (February 14, 2008), http://www.alliancetrends.org/nonprofits.cfm? id=53.

18. Ronald L. and Caryl Rae Krannich, *Jobs and Careers with Non-Profit Organizations* (Manassas Park, VA: Impact Publications, 1998).

Chapter 5

19. Jeff Severns Guntzel, "Lessons for an Activist from a White, Republican Male," *Utne Reader* (February 17, 2009), http://www .utne.com/Spirituality/Lessons-for-an-Activist-from-a-White-Republican-Male.aspx (accessed March 2009).

Chapter 6

20. See charitynavigator.com for more information.

Chapter 7

21. Bill George, "Truly Authentic Leadership," *U.S. News & World Report* (October 22, 2006), http://www.usnews.com/usnews/ news/articles/061022/30authentic_2.htm (accessed April 2009).

22. Merriam-Webster OnLine, s.v. "authentic," http://www.mer riam-webster.com/dictionary/authentic.

Chapter 8

23. Allan Luks, *The Healing Power of Doing Good: The Health and Spiritual Benefits of Helping Others* (Lincoln: iUniverse.com, Inc., 2001), 160.

24. Arthur C. Brooks, "Giving Makes You Rich," *Entrepreneur* (October 17, 2007), http://www.entrepreneur.com/growyourbusiness/portfoliocombusinessnewsandopinion/article185662.html (accessed April 2009).

25. Ibid.

Resources to Get You Started

Over the years, I've read articles, listened to podcasts, and browsed websites searching for the best information, tools, and tips about philanthropy, giving back, and fundraising. While I have not found every website worth reading and learning from, the sites listed here are among the sites I visit most often and from which I have learned a lot. They provide valuable thinking and analysis of the sector, and I count on them to keep me informed and up-to-date.

I often get asked about how you can know if a charitable or social change organization is operating ethically and spending wisely. To assist you in getting an initial snapshot of an organization, I'm also including a list of the most reputable watchdog groups.

I hope these websites and resources serve you well. For more information, please visit kathylemay.com.

Watchdog Organizations

Charity Navigator: charitynavigator.org
Mission: *Charity Navigator works to guide intelligent giving. We help charitable givers make intelligent giving decisions by providing*

information on over five thousand charities and by evaluating the financial health of each of these charities

Guidestar: guidestar.org
Mission: *To revolutionize philanthropy and nonprofit practice by providing information that advances transparency, enables users to make better decisions, and encourages charitable giving*

News, Trends, and Analysis

Chronicle of Philanthropy: philanthropy.com
The Newspaper of the Nonprofit World

Stanford Social Innovation Review: ssir.org
Mission: *To share substantive insights and practical experiences that will help those who do the important work of improving society [to] do it even better*

Volunteer and Giving Opportunities

Idealist: idealist.org
Mission: *A project Action Without Borders that connects people, organizations, and resources to help build a world where all people can live free and dignified lives*

Volunteer Match: volunteermatch.org
Mission: *[To strengthen] communities by making it easier for good people and good causes to connect*

Spirit of Fundraising and Philanthropy

Soul of Money Institute: soulofmoney.org
Mission: *Transforming your relationship with money and life*